Table of Contents

Table of Contents 1
Free Gift 8
Introduction 9
Slow Cooker Breakfast Recipes For 2 10
    Creamy Oatmeal 10
    Breakfast Potatoes Mix 10
    Lovely Quinoa Breakfast Mix 11
    Hash Brown Breakfast 11
    Breakfast Casserole 12
    Creamy Banana Breakfast 12
    Carrots And Zucchini Oatmeal 13
    Tater Tot Casserole 13
    Blueberry And Banana Oatmeal 14
    Light Peanut Butter Oatmeal 14
    Cranberry Oatmeal 15
    Carrot Oatmeal 15
    Apple Pie Oatmeal 16
    Pumpkin Oatmeal 16
    Amazing German Oatmeal 17
    Quinoa Casserole 17
    Tasty Cauliflower Hash Browns 18
    Tasty Breakfast Pie 18
    Baked Egg Casserole 19
    Rich Breakfast Casserole 19
    Shrimp Breakfast Casserole 20
    Peach Bowls 20
    Special Omelet 21
    Delicious Potato Omelet 21
    Kale Frittata 22
    Mexican Frittata 22
    Spinach Breakfast Quiche 23
    Zucchini Frittata 23
    Pumpkin Bread 24
    Easy Banana Bread 24
    Potato Casserole 25
    Pear And Maple Oatmeal 25
    Cheese And Veggies Casserole 26
    Apples And Pears Bowls 26
    Apple And Cashew Butter Bowls 27
    Nuts And Squash Bowls 27
    Pork And Eggs Breakfast Mix 28

- Sausage Casserole 28
- Breakfast Pork Meatloaf 29
- Leek, Kale And Sausage Casserole 29
- Eggs And Bacon Breakfast Mix 30
- Sweet Potato Casserole 30
- Breakfast Pumpkin Spread 31
- Cherry Oats 31
- Beans Breakfast Burrito 32
- Mexican Rice Breakfast 32
- Berry Butter 33
- Pumpkin Butter 33
- Quinoa Pudding 34
- Cornbread Breakfast Mix 34

Slow Cooker Main Dish Recipes For 2 35
- Seafood Chowder 35
- Asian Salmon Fillets 35
- Scallops And Shrimp Stew 36
- Spicy Tuna 36
- Simple Flavored Salmon 37
- Coconut Clams 37
- Clam Chowder 38
- Pulled Chicken 38
- Chicken Chili 39
- Chicken And Mushrooms 39
- Indian Chicken 40
- Turkey With Cherries, Cranberries And Figs 40
- Turkey And Sweet Potatoes 41
- Slow Cooked Chicken 41
- Roasted Beef Chuck 42
- Pork Chops And Pineapple Mix 42
- Pork And Apples 43
- Lamb Stew 43
- Pork Roast And Veggies 44
- Beef Stew 44
- Slow Cooked Beef Stew And Red Wine 45
- Slow Cooked Pasta Dish 45
- Honey Roast 46
- Creamy Beef Mix 46
- Turkey And Chickpeas Stew 47
- Lentils Soup 47
- Slow Cooked Chicken Mix 48
- Lemon Chicken 48
- Tasty Gumbo 49

- Chicken Soup 49
- Italian Pork Loin 50
- Spinach And Mushroom Tortellini 50
- Bacon Chili 51
- French Chicken Dish 51
- BBQ Short Ribs 52
- Smooth Beef Brisket 52
- White Chicken Soup 53
- Potato And Bacon Soup 53
- Delicious Chicken And Rice 54
- Mixed Pork, Beef And Beans 54
- Pork Chops And Creamy Sauce 55
- Balsamic Chicken Mix 55
- Chicken Drumsticks And Blue Cheese Sauce 56
- Mustard Pork Chops 56
- Easy Leeks And Fennel Soup 57
- Beef And Artichoke Soup 57
- Veggie Stew 58
- Eggplant Stew 58
- Lentils Stew 59

Slow Cooker Side Dish Recipes For 2 60
- Creamy Scalloped Tater Tots 60
- Quick Broccoli Side Dish 60
- Delicious Bean Mix 61
- Easy Green Beans Mix 61
- Creamy Corn Side Dish 62
- Tasty Peas And Carrots 62
- Corn Chowder 63
- Mushroom Rice 63
- Butternut Mix 64
- Easy Potatoes Mix 64
- Beans And Spinach Mix 65
- Creamy Potatoes 65
- Sweet Potatoes And Orange Mix 66
- Cauliflower And Broccoli Mix 66
- Mushroom Risotto 67
- Curried Veggie Side Dish 67
- Rosemary Potatoes 68
- Maple And Thyme Brussels Sprouts 68
- Potatoes And Apples Mix 69
- Chili Black Beans Mix 69
- Simple Carrots Mix 70
- Hot Beans And Lentils 70

Wild Rice Mix 71
Mashed Potatoes 71
Squash Mix 72
Beans And Sauce 72
Hot Beans 73
Flavored Potato And Spinach Mix 73
Baked Beans 74
White Bean Mix 74
Mixed Veggies Side Dish 75
Cabbage And Apples Mix 75
Flavored Mushroom Mix 76
Squash And Sauce 76
Zucchini And Squash Mix 77
Simple Kale Side Dish 77
Cheesy Spinach 78
Simple Sweet Potatoes Mix 78
Cauliflower Mash 79
Veggie Mix 79
Rice And Farro Pilaf 80
Quinoa Pilaf 80
Moroccan Risotto 81
Farro Pilaf 81
Parmesan And Peas Rice 82
Spinach And Cheese Rice 82
Pineapple Rice 83
Simple Artichokes 83
Simple Bok Choy 84
Italian Eggplant Mix 84

Slow Cooker Appetizer And Snack Recipes For 2 85
Artichokes Party Spread 85
Caesar Artichoke Dip 85
Crab And Artichoke Spread 86
Cheesy Crab Dip 86
Squash Spread 87
Cashew Spread 87
Veggie Party Rolls 88
Veggie Spread 88
Italian Veggie Dip 89
Hummus 89
Spinach Dip 90
Potato Salad 90
Stuffed Bell Peppers 91
Corn Dip 91

- Cheesy Mushroom Salsa 92
- Refried Beans Spread 92
- Thai Tofu Party Mix 93
- Chickpeas Appetizer Salad 93
- Creamy Mushroom Appetizer 94
- Bulgur Appetizer Salad 94
- Root Veggie Salad 95
- Lentils Sloppy Joe 95
- Easy And Tasty Tacos 96
- Almond Snack 96
- Eggplant Salsa 97
- Almond And Beans Spread 97
- Onion Dip 98
- Simple Nuts Snack 98
- Eggplant Appetizer Salad 99
- Lentils Dip 99
- Beef Party Meatballs 100
- Stuffed Jalapenos 100
- Fish Sticks 101
- Easy Pecans Snack 101
- Sausage Bites 102
- Spinach Spread 102
- Beef Cakes 103
- Squid Appetizer 103
- Seafood Salad 104
- Stuffed Chicken Appetizer 104
- Apple Dip 105
- Sweet Potato Dip 105
- Squash Salad 106
- Chicken Meatballs 106
- Pecans Snack 107
- Seasoned Peanuts 107
- Cauliflower Dip 108
- Walnuts And Pumpkin Seeds Snack 108
- Mini Sausages Snack 109
- Chicken Dip 109

Slow Cooker Dessert Recipes For 2 110
- Stuffed Apples 110
- Sweet Apples And Cane Juice 110
- Banana Cake 111
- Coconut And Chocolate Cream 111
- Winter Pudding 112
- Cherry And Cocoa Compote 112

- Berry And Cashew Cake ... 113
- Cashew And Coconut Pudding ... 113
- Simple Citrus Pudding ... 114
- Creamy Apples ... 114
- Cinnamon Plum Compote ... 115
- Apple Cake ... 115
- Peach Cobbler ... 116
- Blueberry And Almond Cake ... 116
- Pears And Sauce ... 117
- Almond Cookies ... 117
- Strawberries And Raisins Marmalade ... 118
- Easy Lemon Jam ... 118
- Cinnamon Rice Pudding ... 119
- Blueberry Pudding ... 119
- Almond And Mandarin Pudding ... 120
- Cinnamon Rolls ... 120
- Sweet Plums ... 121
- Plum Cream ... 121
- Sweet Rhubarb Mix ... 122
- Peaches And Special Sauce ... 122
- Apricot Jam ... 123
- Black Grapes Dessert ... 123
- Pomegranate Jam ... 124
- Sweet Orange Cream ... 124
- Cranberries And Clementine Cream ... 125
- Sweet Pineapple Mix ... 125
- Strawberry Mix ... 126
- Cranberry Mix ... 126
- Sweet Melon Dessert ... 127
- Chocolate Cheesecake ... 127
- Chocolate Cream ... 128
- Tasty Blackberry Jam ... 128
- Spiced Peach Jam ... 129
- Rhubarb Jam ... 129
- Strawberry Jam ... 130
- Pear And Honey Jam ... 130
- Lingo berry Jam ... 131
- Strawberry And Jalapeno Marmalade ... 131
- Spicy Tomato Jam ... 132
- Chili Jam ... 132
- Onion Jam ... 133
- Different Tomato Jam ... 133
- Bread Pudding ... 134

    Tapioca Pudding 134
Conclusion 135
Recipe Index... 136

Free Gift

I also have one valuable bonus for you - 1000 Worldwide Recipes - cookbook

Please follow this link to get instant access to your Free Cookbook:
http://booknation.top/

Introduction

Do you love cooking for your loved one? Are you always looking for the best recipes to prepare for you and your partner?
We know you do and that's why we thought you could use such a cooking journal.
We searched for the best and most delicious recipes for you to cook for a romantic occasion but also for the easiest cooking method and we've come up with this next cookbook!
That's how we developed a slow cooker recipes collection for 2!

Slow cookers are so popular all over the world these days and more and more people use them every day!
These wonderful kitchen tools help you prepare hearty and rich meals, full of flavors and textures.
The best thing about these tools is that you don't really have to do much. You just need the right ingredients and to combine them in the right order!
Your slow cooker will do the rest!

So, if you are passionate about special and delightful recipes and if you want to prepare them for your loved one, then you should really consider using these next recipes!
Trust us! You and your slow cooker will make wonders in the kitchen and your loved one will appreciate you even more!

So, let's start our amazing culinary journey right away!
Have fun cooking recipes for 2 in your slow cooker!

Slow Cooker Breakfast Recipes For 2

Creamy Oatmeal

Preparation time: 10 minutes
Cooking time: 6 hours
Servings: 2

Ingredients:
- 1 cup steel cut oats
- 3 cups water
- 1 cup almond milk
- 1 cup strawberries, chopped
- ½ cup Greek yogurt
- ½ teaspoon cinnamon powder
- ½ teaspoon vanilla extract

Directions:
In your slow cooker, mix oats with water, milk, strawberries, yogurt, cinnamon and vanilla, toss, cover and cook on Low for 6 hours. Stir your oatmeal one more time, divide into bowls and serve for breakfast.
Enjoy!

Nutrition: calories 201, fat 3, fiber 6, carbs 12, protein 6

Breakfast Potatoes Mix

Preparation time: 10 minutes
Cooking time: 4 hours
Servings: 2

Ingredients:
- 1 potato, chopped
- ½ red bell pepper, chopped
- ½ green bell pepper, chopped
- ½ yellow onion, chopped
- 4 ounces smoked andouille sausage, sliced
- 1 cup cheddar cheese, shredded
- ¼ cup sour cream
- A pinch of oregano, dried
- ¼ teaspoon basil, dried
- 4 ounces chicken cream
- Salt and black pepper to the taste
- 1 tablespoon parsley, chopped

Directions:
Put the potato in your slow cooker, add red bell pepper, green bell pepper, onion, sausage, cheese, sour cream, oregano, basil, salt, pepper and chicken cream, cover and cook on Low for 4 hours. Add parsley, toss, divide between plates and serve for breakfast.
Enjoy!

Nutrition: calories 355, fat 14, fiber 4, carbs 20, protein 22

Lovely Quinoa Breakfast Mix

Preparation time: 10 minutes
Cooking time: 8 hours
Servings: 2

Ingredients:
- ½ cup quinoa
- 1 cup water
- ½ cup coconut milk
- 1 tablespoon maple syrup
- A pinch of salt
- 1 tablespoon berries

Directions:
In your slow cooker, mix quinoa with water, coconut milk, maple syrup and salt, stir well, cover and cook on Low for 8 hours. Divide into 2 bowls, sprinkle berries on top and serve for breakfast. Enjoy!

Nutrition: calories 261, fat 5, fiber 7, carbs 12, protein 5

Hash Brown Breakfast

Preparation time: 10 minutes
Cooking time: 3 hours
Servings: 2

Ingredients:
- 1 tablespoon butter
- 2 tablespoons mushrooms, chopped
- 2 tablespoons yellow onion, chopped
- ¼ teaspoon garlic powder
- 1 tablespoon flour
- ½ cup milk
- ¼ cup sour cream
- 10 ounces hash browns
- ¼ cup cheddar cheese, shredded
- Salt and black pepper to the taste
- ½ tablespoon parsley, chopped
- Cooking spray

Directions:
Heat up a pan with the butter over medium heat, add onion and mushroom, garlic powder and flour, stir and cook for 1 minute. Add milk gradually, stir, cook until it thickens and take off heat. Grease your slow cooker with cooking spray and add mushrooms mix. Add hash browns, sour cream, cheddar cheese, salt and pepper, cover and cook on High for 3 hours. Divide between plates and serve right away for breakfast with parsley sprinkled on top
Enjoy!

Nutrition: calories 245, fat 4, fiber 7, carbs 7, protein 10

Breakfast Casserole

Preparation time: 10 minutes
Cooking time: 3 hours
Servings: 2

Ingredients:
- 5 ounces hash browns, shredded
- 2 bacon slices, cooked and chopped
- 2 ounces cheddar cheese, shredded
- 3 eggs, whisked
- 1 green onion, chopped
- ¼ cup milk
- Cooking spray
- A pinch of salt and black pepper

Directions:
Grease your slow cooker with cooking spray and add hash browns, bacon and cheese. In a bowl, mix eggs with green onion, milk, salt and pepper, whisk well and add to slow cooker. Cover, cook on High for 3 hours, divide between plates and serve.
Enjoy!

Nutrition: calories 281, fat 4, fiber 6, carbs 12, protein 11

Creamy Banana Breakfast

Preparation time: 10 minutes
Cooking time: 4 hours
Servings: 2

Ingredients:
- ½ French baguette, sliced
- 2 bananas, sliced
- 2 ounces cream cheese
- 1 tablespoon brown sugar
- ¼ cup walnuts, chopped
- 1 egg, whisked
- 3 tablespoons skim milk
- 2 tablespoons honey
- ½ teaspoon cinnamon powder
- A pinch of nutmeg, ground
- ¼ teaspoon vanilla extract
- 1 tablespoon butter
- Cooking spray

Directions:
Spread cream cheese on all bread slices and grease your slow cooker with cooking spray. Arrange bread slices in your slow cooker, layer banana slices, brown sugar and walnuts. In a bowl, mix eggs with skim milk, honey, cinnamon, nutmeg and vanilla extract, whisk and add over bread slices. Add butter, cover, cook on Low for 4 hours, divide between plates and serve for breakfast.
Enjoy!

Nutrition: calories 251, fat 5, fiber 7, carbs 12, protein 4

Carrots and Zucchini Oatmeal

Preparation time: 10 minutes
Cooking time: 8 hours
Servings: 2

Ingredients:

- ½ cup steel cut oats
- 1 cup coconut milk
- 1 carrot, grated
- ¼ zucchini, grated
- A pinch of nutmeg, ground
- A pinch of cloves, ground
- ½ teaspoon cinnamon powder
- 2 tablespoons brown sugar
- ¼ cup pecans, chopped
- Cooking spray

Directions:
Grease your slow cooker with cooking spray, add oats, milk, carrot, zucchini, nutmeg, cloves, cinnamon and sugar, toss, cover and cook on Low for 8 hours. Divide into 2 bowls, sprinkle pecans on top and serve.
Enjoy!

Nutrition: calories 200, fat 4, fiber 8, carbs 11, protein 5

Tater Tot Casserole

Preparation time: 10 minutes
Cooking time: 4 hours
Servings: 2

Ingredients:

- Cooking spray
- 10 ounces tater tots, frozen
- 2 eggs, whisked
- ½ pound turkey sausage, ground
- 1 tablespoon heavy cream
- ¼ teaspoon thyme, dried
- ¼ teaspoon garlic powder
- A pinch of salt and black pepper
- ½ cup Colby jack cheese, shredded

Directions:
Grease your slow cooker with cooking spray, spread tater tots on the bottom, add sausage, thyme, garlic powder, salt, pepper and whisked eggs. Add cheese, cover pot and cook on Low for 4 hours. Divide between plates and serve for breakfast.
Enjoy!

Nutrition: calories 231, fat 5, fiber 9, carbs 15, protein 11

Blueberry and Banana Oatmeal

Preparation time: 10 minutes
Cooking time: 6 hours
Servings: 2

Ingredients:
- 1/2 cup steel cut oats
- ¼ cup quinoa
- ½ cup blueberries
- 1 banana, mashed
- A pinch of cinnamon powder
- 2 tablespoons maple syrup
- 2 cups water
- Cooking spray
- ½ cup coconut milk

Directions:
Grease your slow cooker with cooking spray, add oats, quinoa, blueberries, banana, cinnamon, maple syrup, water and coconut milk, stir, cover and cook on Low for 6 hours. Divide into 2 bowls and serve for breakfast.
Enjoy!

Nutrition: calories 200, fat 4, fiber 5, carbs 8, protein 5

Light Peanut Butter Oatmeal

Preparation time: 10 minutes
Cooking time: 8 hours
Servings: 2

Ingredients:
- 1 banana, mashed
- 1 and ½ cups almond milk
- ½ cup steel cut oats
- 2 tablespoons peanut butter
- ½ teaspoon vanilla extract
- ½ teaspoon cinnamon powder
- ½ tablespoon chia seeds

Directions:
In your slow cooker, mix almond milk with banana, oats, peanut butter, vanilla extract, cinnamon and chia, stir, cover and cook on Low for 8 hours. Stir oatmeal one more time, divide into 2 bowls and serve.
Enjoy!

Nutrition: calories 222, fat 5, fiber 6, carbs 9, protein 11

Cranberry Oatmeal

Preparation time: 10 minutes
Cooking time: 3 hours
Servings: 2

Ingredients:
- Cooking spray
- 2 cups water
- 1 cup old fashioned oats
- ¼ cup cranberries, dried
- 1 apple, chopped
- 1 tablespoon butter, melted
- ½ teaspoon cinnamon powder

Directions:
Grease your slow cooker with cooking spray, add water, oats, cranberries, apple, butter and cinnamon, stir well, cover and cook on Low for 3 hours. Stir oatmeal again, divide into bowls and serve for breakfast.
Enjoy!

Nutrition: calories 182, fat 4, fiber 6, carbs 8, protein 10

Carrot Oatmeal

Preparation time: 10 minutes
Cooking time: 8 hours
Servings: 2

Ingredients:
- ½ cup water
- ½ cup coconut milk
- ½ cup steel cut oats
- ½ cup carrots, grated
- ¼ cup raisins
- A pinch of cinnamon powder
- A pinch of ginger, ground
- A pinch of nutmeg, ground
- ¼ cup coconut flakes, shredded
- 1 tablespoon orange zest, grated
- ½ teaspoon vanilla extract
- ½ tablespoon maple syrup
- 2 tablespoons walnuts, chopped

Directions:
In your slow cooker, mix water with coconut milk, oats, carrots, raisins, cinnamon, ginger, nutmeg, coconut flakes, orange zest, vanilla extract and maple syrup, stir, cover and cook on Low for 8 hours. Add walnuts, stir, divide into 2 bowls and serve for breakfast.
Enjoy!

Nutrition: calories 200, fat 4, fiber 6, carbs 8, protein 8

Apple Pie Oatmeal

Preparation time: 10 minutes
Cooking time: 8 hours
Servings: 2

Ingredients:
- ½ cup steel cut oats
- 1 apple, chopped
- 1 cup apple juice
- 1 cup milk
- 2 tablespoons maple syrup
- 1 teaspoon vanilla extract
- ½ tablespoon cinnamon powder
- A pinch of nutmeg, ground
- Cooking spray

Directions:
Grease your slow cooker with the cooking spray, add oats, apple, apple juice, milk, maple syrup, vanilla extract, cinnamon and nutmeg, stir, cover and cook on Low for 8 hours. Stir oatmeal one more time, divide into bowls and serve.
Enjoy!

Nutrition: calories 221, fat 4, fiber 6, carbs 8, protein 10

Pumpkin Oatmeal

Preparation time: 10 minutes
Cooking time: 7 hours
Servings: 2

Ingredients:
- Cooking spray
- ½ cup steel cut oats
- 1 cup water
- 1 cup almond milk
- 1 and ½ tablespoon maple syrup
- ½ teaspoon vanilla extract
- ½ teaspoon pumpkin pie spice
- ½ cup pumpkin, chopped
- ¼ teaspoon cinnamon powder

Directions:
Grease your slow cooker with cooking spray, add steel cut oats, water, almond milk, maple syrup, vanilla, pumpkin spice, pumpkin and cinnamon, stir, cover and cook on Low for 7 hours. Stir one more time, divide into bowls and serve.
Enjoy!

Nutrition: calories 242, fat 3, fiber 8, carbs 20, protein 7

Amazing German Oatmeal

Preparation time: 10 minutes
Cooking time: 8 hours
Servings: 2

Ingredients:
- Cooking spray
- 1 cup steel cut oats
- 3 cups water
- 6 ounces coconut milk
- 2 tablespoons cocoa powder
- 1 tablespoon brown sugar
- 1 tablespoon coconut, shredded

Directions:
Grease your slow cooker with cooking spray, add oats, water, milk, cocoa powder, sugar and shredded coconut, stir, cover and cook on Low for 8 hours. Stir oatmeal one more time, divide into 2 bowls and serve for breakfast.
Enjoy!

Nutrition: calories 200, fat 4, fiber 5, carbs 17, protein 5

Quinoa Casserole

Preparation time: 10 minutes
Cooking time: 4 hours
Servings: 2

Ingredients:
- ¼ cup quinoa
- 1 cup milk
- 2 eggs
- A pinch of salt and black pepper
- ¼ cup spinach, chopped
- ¼ cup cherry tomatoes, halved
- 2 tablespoons cheddar cheese, shredded
- 2 tablespoons parmesan, shredded
- Cooking spray

Directions:
In a bowl, mix eggs with quinoa, milk, salt, pepper, tomatoes, spinach and cheddar cheese and whisk well. Grease your slow cooker with cooking spray, add eggs and quinoa mix, spread parmesan all over, cover and cook on High for 4 hours. Divide between plates and serve.
Enjoy!

Nutrition: calories 251, fat 5, fiber 7, carbs 19, protein 11

Tasty Cauliflower Hash Browns

Preparation time: 10 minutes
Cooking time: 7 hours
Servings: 2

Ingredients:
- Cooking spray
- ½ cup milk
- 3 eggs, whisked
- A pinch of salt and black pepper
- ¼ teaspoon dried mustard
- ½ cauliflower head, shredded
- ½ small yellow onion, chopped
- 3 ounces breakfast sausages, sliced
- ½ cup cheddar cheese, shredded

Directions:
Grease your slow cooker with cooking spray and spread cauliflower on the bottom. Add onion, sausage, salt, pepper and mustard. In a bowl, mix eggs with milk, salt and pepper, whisk and pour over cauliflower mix. Sprinkle cheese at the end, cover pot and cook on Low for 7 hours. Slice and serve for breakfast.
Enjoy!

Nutrition: calories 261, fat 6, fiber 7, carbs 22, protein 6

Tasty Breakfast Pie

Preparation time: 10 minutes
Cooking time: 8 hours
Servings: 2

Ingredients:
- 4 eggs, whisked
- ½ sweet potato, shredded
- ½ pound pork sausage, sliced
- ½ yellow onion, chopped
- ½ tablespoon garlic powder
- 1 teaspoon basil, dried
- A pinch of salt and black pepper
- Cooking spray

Directions:
Grease your slow cooker with cooking spray, add potato, sausage, onion, garlic powder, basil, salt and pepper and toss. Add whisked eggs, toss everything, cover and cook on Low for 8 hours. Divide between plates and serve right away for breakfast.
Enjoy!

Nutrition: calories 271, fat 7, fiber 8, carbs 20, protein 11

Baked Egg Casserole

Preparation time: 10 minutes
Cooking time: 8 hours
Servings: 2

Ingredients:
- 6 ounces tater tots
- 2 ounces bacon, chopped
- 1 yellow onion, chopped
- ½ cup cheddar cheese, shredded
- 3 eggs
- ¼ cup milk
- 2 tablespoons parmesan
- 1 tablespoon flour
- Salt and black pepper to the taste
- Cooking spray

Directions:
Grease your slow cooker with the cooking spray and spread tater tots on the bottom of the pot. Add bacon, onion and cheddar cheese. In a bowl, mix eggs with milk, flour, salt and pepper, whisk really well and pour over tater tots mix. Sprinkle parmesan, cover, cook on Low for 8 hours, divide between plates and serve for breakfast.
Enjoy!

Nutrition: calories 261, fat 6, fiber 8, carbs 26, protein 11

Rich Breakfast Casserole

Preparation time: 10 minutes
Cooking time: 4 hours
Servings: 2

Ingredients:
- 2 eggs
- 1 egg white
- ½ teaspoon mustard
- A pinch of salt and black pepper
- 6 ounces hash browns
- 1 bacon strip, cooked and chopped
- 1 small red onion, chopped
- ½ red bell pepper, chopped
- 1 ounce cheddar cheese, shredded
- A drizzle of olive oil
- ½ small broccoli head, florets separated and chopped

Directions:
Grease your slow cooker with a drizzle of oil and spread hash browns, bacon, onion, broccoli and bell pepper on the bottom. In a bowl, mix eggs with egg white, mustard, salt and pepper and whisk well. Pour this over veggies, cover, cook on Low for 4 hours, divide between plates and serve for breakfast.
Enjoy!

Nutrition: calories 261, fat 7, fiber 8, carbs 20, protein 11

Shrimp Breakfast Casserole

Preparation time: 10 minutes
Cooking time: 3 hours and 30 minutes
Servings: 2

Ingredients:
- 2 cups chicken stock
- 1 cup cooking grits
- ¼ tablespoon garlic powder
- ¼ tablespoon onion powder
- ¼ teaspoon thyme, dried
- A pinch of salt and black pepper
- ¼ cup cheddar cheese, shredded
- 1 ounce cream cheese
- 2 tablespoons parmesan, grated
- ½ pound shrimp, peeled and deveined
- 1 tablespoon chives, chopped

Directions:
In your slow cooker, mix stock with grits, garlic powder, onion powder, thyme, salt, pepper, cheddar and cream cheese, stir, cover and cook on Low for 3 hours. Add shrimp and parmesan, stir, cover and cook on Low for 30 minutes more. Divide into bowls, sprinkle chives and serve for breakfast.
Enjoy!

Nutrition: calories 300, fat 7, fiber 12, carbs 20, protein 10

Peach Bowls

Preparation time: 10 minutes
Cooking time: 8 hours
Servings: 2

Ingredients:
- ½ cup steel cut oats
- 4 cups water
- ½ pound peaches, pitted and roughly chopped
- ½ teaspoon vanilla extract
- 1 cup blueberries
- 1 teaspoon cinnamon powder

Directions:
In your slow cooker, mix oats with water, peaches, vanilla, blueberries and cinnamon, stir, cover and cook on Low for 8 hours. Divide into bowls and serve for breakfast right away.
Enjoy!

Nutrition: calories 261, fat 5, fiber 8, carbs 18, protein 6

Special Omelet

Preparation time: 10 minutes
Cooking time: 2 hours
Servings: 2

Ingredients:
- Cooking spray
- 3 eggs, whisked
- ¼ cup milk
- A pinch of salt and black pepper
- A pinch of garlic powder
- A pinch of chili powder
- ½ cup broccoli florets
- ½ red bell pepper, chopped
- ½ yellow onion, chopped
- 1 small garlic clove, minced
- 1 tomato, chopped
- 1 tablespoon parsley, chopped

Directions:
In a bowl, mix eggs with milk, salt, pepper, chili powder, garlic powder, broccoli, bell pepper, onion and garlic and whisk really well. Grease your slow cooker with cooking spray, pour eggs mix, spread, cover and cook on High for 2 hours. Slice into halves, divide omelet between plates, sprinkle tomato and parsley on top and serve for breakfast.
Enjoy!

Nutrition: calories 162, fat 5, fiber 7, carbs 15, protein 4

Delicious Potato Omelet

Preparation time: 10 minutes
Cooking time: 6 hours
Servings: 2

Ingredients:
- Cooking spray
- 2 eggs
- ½ cup red potatoes, chopped
- ¼ cup milk
- ¼ cup ham, chopped
- Salt and black pepper to the taste

Directions:
In a bowl, mix eggs with potatoes, milk, ham, salt and pepper and whisk well. Grease your slow cooker with cooking spray, add eggs and potato mix, spread, cover and cook on Low for 6 hours. Slice your omelet into halves, divide between plates and serve.
Enjoy!

Nutrition: calories 200, fat 4, fiber 6, carbs 12, protein 6

Kale Frittata

Preparation time: 10 minutes
Cooking time: 3 hours
Servings: 2

Ingredients:
- 1 teaspoon olive oil
- 3 ounces kale
- 3 ounces roasted red peppers, drained and chopped
- 2 tablespoons green onions, chopped
- 2 ounces feta cheese, crumbled
- 3 eggs, whisked
- A pinch of spike seasoning
- A pinch of salt and black pepper

Directions:
Heat up a pan with the oil over medium heat, add kale, stir, cook for a couple of minutes and transfer to your slow cooker. Add red peppers and green onions to your slow cooker as well. In a bowl, mix eggs with spike seasoning, salt and pepper and whisk well. Spread this into the pot, sprinkle cheese, cover and cook on Low for 3 hours. Slice omelet into halves, divide between plates and serve.
Enjoy!

Nutrition: calories 251, fat 4, fiber 6, carbs 12, protein 5

Mexican Frittata

Preparation time: 10 minutes
Cooking time: 3 hours
Servings: 2

Ingredients:
- Cooking spray
- ½ red onion, chopped
- ½ red bell pepper, chopped
- 2 tablespoons sun dried tomatoes, chopped
- 1 ounce canned and roasted green chili pepper, chopped
- ½ teaspoon oregano, dried
- 1 teaspoon skim milk
- Salt and black pepper to the taste
- 3 ounces cheddar cheese, shredded
- 4 eggs, whisked

Directions:
Grease your slow cooker with cooking spray and spread onion, bell pepper, sun dried tomatoes and green chilies on the bottom. In a bowl, mix eggs with skim milk, salt and pepper. Pour this over mixed veggies in the pot, sprinkle cheddar all over, cover pot and cook on Low for 3 hours. Slice in halves, divide between plates and serve.
Enjoy!

Nutrition: calories 224, fat 4, fiber 7, carbs 18, protein 11

Spinach Breakfast Quiche

Preparation time: 10 minutes
Cooking time: 4 hours
Servings: 2

Ingredients:
- 2 eggs
- 1 cup milk
- 2 ounces feta cheese, crumbled
- 5 ounces spinach, chopped
- A pinch of salt and black pepper
- Cooking spray

Directions:
In a bowl, mix eggs with milk, cheese, spinach, salt and pepper and whisk well. Grease your slow cooker with cooking spray, add eggs mix, spread, cover and cook on Low for 4 hours. Divide between plates and serve for breakfast.
Enjoy!

Nutrition: calories 214, fat 4, fiber 7, carbs 18, protein 5

Zucchini Frittata

Preparation time: 10 minutes
Cooking time: 3 hours
Servings: 2

Ingredients:
- Cooking spray
- 2 eggs
- 1 zucchini, grated
- ¼ teaspoon sweet paprika
- ¼ teaspoon thyme, dried
- A pinch of salt and black pepper
- 1 and ½ tablespoon parsley, chopped
- 1 tablespoon feta cheese, crumbled
- 4 cherry tomatoes, halved

Directions:
In a bowl, mix eggs with zucchini, paprika, thyme, salt, pepper, cheese, parsley and tomatoes and whisk. Grease your slow cooker with cooking spray, pour frittata mix, cover and cook on Low for 3 hours. Divide between plates and serve for breakfast.
Enjoy!

Nutrition: calories 261, fat 5, fiber 7, carbs 19, protein 6

Pumpkin Bread

Preparation time: 10 minutes
Cooking time: 2 hours
Servings: 2

Ingredients:
- Cooking spray
- ½ cup white flour
- ½ cup whole wheat flour
- ½ teaspoon baking soda
- A pinch of cinnamon powder
- 2 tablespoons olive oil
- 2 tablespoons maple syrup
- 1 egg
- ½ tablespoon milk
- ½ teaspoon vanilla extract
- ½ cup pumpkin puree
- 2 tablespoons walnuts, chopped
- 2 tablespoons chocolate chips

Directions:
In a bowl, mix white flour with whole wheat flour, baking soda and cinnamon and stir. Add maple syrup, olive oil, egg, milk, vanilla extract, pumpkin puree, walnuts and chocolate chips and stir well. Grease a loaf pan that fits your slow cooker with cooking spray, pour pumpkin bread, transfer to your cooker and cook on High for 2 hours. Slice bread, divide between plates and serve.
Enjoy!

Nutrition: calories 200, fat 3, fiber 5, carbs 8, protein 4

Easy Banana Bread

Preparation time: 10 minutes
Cooking time: 4 hours
Servings: 2

Ingredients:
- 1 egg
- 2 tablespoons butter, melted
- ½ cup sugar
- 1 cup flour
- ½ teaspoon baking powder
- ¼ teaspoon baking soda
- A pinch of cinnamon powder
- A pinch of nutmeg, ground
- 2 bananas, mashed
- ¼ cup almonds, sliced
- Cooking spray

Directions:
In a bowl, mix sugar with flour, baking powder, baking soda, cinnamon and nutmeg and stir. Add egg, butter, almonds and bananas and stir really well. Grease your slow cooker with cooking spray, pour bread mix, cover and cook on Low for 4 hours. Slice bread and serve for breakfast.
Enjoy!

Nutrition: calories 211, fat 3, fiber 6, carbs 12, protein 5

Potato Casserole

Preparation time: 10 minutes
Cooking time: 3 hours and 30 minutes
Servings: 2

Ingredients:
- 1 teaspoon onion powder
- 2 eggs, whisked
- ½ teaspoon garlic powder
- ½ teaspoon sage, dried
- Salt and black pepper to the taste
- ½ yellow onion, chopped
- 1 tablespoons parsley, chopped
- 2 garlic cloves, minced
- A pinch of red pepper flakes
- ½ tablespoon olive oil
- 2 red potatoes, cubed

Directions:
Grease your slow cooker with the oil, add potatoes, onion, garlic, parsley and pepper flakes and toss a bit. In a bowl, mix eggs with onion powder, garlic powder, sage, salt and pepper, whisk well and pour over potatoes. Cover, cook on High for 3 hours and 30 minutes, divide into 2 plates and serve for breakfast.
Enjoy!

Nutrition: calories 218, fat 6, fiber 6, carbs 14, protein 5

Pear And Maple Oatmeal

Preparation time: 10 minutes
Cooking time: 7 hours
Servings: 2

Ingredients:
- 1 and ½ cups milk
- ½ cup steel cut oats
- ½ teaspoon vanilla extract
- 1 pear, chopped
- ½ teaspoon maple extract
- 1 tablespoon sugar

Directions:
In your slow cooker, combine milk with oats, vanilla, pear, maple extract and sugar, stir, cover and cook on Low for 7 hours. Divide into bowls and serve for breakfast.
Enjoy!

Nutrition: calories 200, fat 5, fiber 7, carbs 14, protein 4

Cheese and Veggies Casserole

Preparation time: 10 minutes
Cooking time: 4 hours
Servings: 2

Ingredients:
- ½ teaspoon lemon zest, grated
- 3 ounces feta cheese, crumbled
- ½ tablespoon lemon juice
- 2 eggs, whisked
- ½ tablespoon apple cider vinegar
- ½ tablespoon olive oil
- 1 garlic cloves, minced
- 4 ounces spinach, torn
- 2 tablespoons yellow onion, chopped
- ¼ teaspoon basil, dried
- 3 ounces mushrooms, sliced
- Salt and black pepper to the taste
- A pinch of red pepper flakes
- Cooking spray

Directions:
In a bowl, mix eggs with lemon zest, lemon juice, vinegar, olive oil, garlic, spinach, onion, basil, mushrooms, salt, pepper, pepper flakes, and whisk well. Grease your slow cooker with cooking spray, add eggs mix, sprinkle cheese all over, cover and cook on Low for 4 hours. Divide between plates and serve for breakfast.
Enjoy!

Nutrition: calories 216, fat 6, fiber 8, carbs 12, protein 4

Apples and Pears Bowls

Preparation time: 10 minutes
Cooking time: 6 hours
Servings: 2

Ingredients:
- 2 apples, cored, peeled and cut into medium chunks
- ½ teaspoon lemon juice
- 2 pears, cored, peeled and cut into medium chunks
- 2 teaspoons sugar
- ¼ teaspoon cinnamon powder
- ½ teaspoon vanilla extract
- ¼ teaspoon ginger, ground
- ¼ teaspoon cloves, ground
- ¼ teaspoon cardamom, ground

Directions:
In your slow cooker, mix apples with pears, lemon juice, sugar, cinnamon, vanilla extract, ginger, cloves and cardamom, stir, cover and cook on Low for 6 hours. Divide into bowls and serve for breakfast.
Enjoy!

Nutrition: calories 201, fat 3, fiber 7, carbs 19, protein 4

Apple and Cashew Butter Bowls

Preparation time: 10 minutes
Cooking time: 4 hours
Servings: 2

Ingredients:
- ½ cup granola
- ½ cup rolled oats
- 2 green apples, cored, peeled and roughly chopped
- ¼ cup apple juice
- 1/8 cup maple syrup
- 2 tablespoons cashew butter
- 1 teaspoon cinnamon powder
- ½ teaspoon nutmeg, ground

Directions:
In your slow cooker, mix granola with oats, apples, apple juice, maple syrup, cashew butter, cinnamon and nutmeg, toss, cover and cook on Low for 4 hours. Divide into bowls and serve for breakfast.
Enjoy!

Nutrition: calories 218, fat 6, fiber 9, carbs 17, protein 6

Nuts and Squash Bowls

Preparation time: 10 minutes
Cooking time: 8 hours
Servings: 2

Ingredients:
- ¼ cup almonds, chopped
- ¼ cup walnuts, chopped
- 1 apple, peeled, cored and cubed
- ½ butternut squash, peeled and cubed
- ½ teaspoon cinnamon powder
- ½ tablespoon sugar
- ¼ teaspoon nutmeg, ground
- ½ cup milk

Directions:
In your slow cooker, mix almond with walnuts, apple, squash, cinnamon, sugar, nutmeg and milk, stir, cover and cook on Low for 8 hours. Divide into bowls and serve.
Enjoy!

Nutrition: calories 140, fat 1, fiber 2, carbs 2, protein 5

Pork and Eggs Breakfast Mix

Preparation time: 10 minutes
Cooking time: 8 hours
Servings: 4

Ingredients:
- ½ pork butt
- ½ teaspoon coriander, ground
- ½ tablespoon oregano, dried
- ½ tablespoon cumin powder
- 1 tablespoon chili powder
- 1 yellow onion, chopped
- A pinch of salt and black pepper
- ½ teaspoon lime juice
- 2 fried eggs
- 1 avocado, peeled, pitted and sliced

Directions:
In a bowl, mix pork butt with coriander, oregano, cumin, chili powder, onion, salt and black pepper, rub, transfer to your slow cooker, cook on Low for 8 hours, shred and divide between 2 plates. Add fried eggs on the side, avocado pieces on top and drizzle limejuice all over. Enjoy!

Nutrition: calories 220, fat 2, fiber 2, carbs 6, protein 2

Sausage Casserole

Preparation time: 10 minutes
Cooking time: 5 hours
Servings: 2

Ingredients:
- ¼ broccoli head, florets separated
- 3 eggs, whisked
- 4 ounces sausages, cooked and sliced
- 1 garlic clove, minced
- A pinch of salt and black pepper
- Cooking spray

Directions:
Spray your slow cooker with the cooking spray; add half of the broccoli, half of the sausages, the garlic and half of the eggs. Season with salt and pepper, layer the rest of the broccoli, sausage and eggs, cover and cook on Low for 5 hours. Slice, divide between 2 plates and serve for breakfast. Enjoy!

Nutrition: calories 200, fat 3, fiber 6, carbs 13, protein 8

Breakfast Pork Meatloaf

Preparation time: 10 minutes
Cooking time: 3 hours
Servings: 2

Ingredients:
- ½ yellow onion, chopped
- 1 pound pork, minced
- ½ teaspoon red pepper flakes
- ½ teaspoon olive oil
- 1 garlic clove, minced
- 2 tablespoons white flour
- ½ teaspoon oregano, chopped
- ½ tablespoon sage, minced
- A pinch of salt and black pepper
- ½ tablespoon sweet paprika
- ½ teaspoon marjoram, dried
- 1 egg

Directions:
In a bowl, mix pork with salt, pepper, onion, garlic, pepper flakes, flour, oregano, sage, paprika, marjoram and egg, stir well and shape your meatloaf. Grease a loaf pan that fits your slow cooker with the oil, add meatloaf mix, spread well, transfer the pan to your slow cooker, cover and cook on Low for 3 hours. Leave aside to cool down, slice and serve for breakfast.
Enjoy!

Nutrition: calories 200, fat 6, fiber 12, carbs 17, protein 10

Leek, Kale and Sausage Casserole

Preparation time: 10 minutes
Cooking time: 4 hours
Servings: 2

Ingredients:
- 1 cup leek, chopped
- 1 tablespoon olive oil
- 1 teaspoon garlic, minced
- ½ cup kale, chopped
- 4 eggs, whisked
- 1 cup beef sausage, chopped
- ½ sweet potatoes, grated

Directions:
Heat up a pan with the oil over medium-high heat, add garlic, leek and kale, stir, cook for a couple of minutes and take off heat. In a bowl, mix eggs with sausage, sweet potato and sautéed veggies, stir well, transfer everything to your slow cooker, cover and cook on Low for 4 hours. Divide between plates and serve for breakfast.
Enjoy!

Nutrition: calories 232, fat 4, fiber 8, carbs 17, protein 4

Eggs and Bacon Breakfast Mix

Preparation time: 10 minutes
Cooking time: 8 hours
Servings: 2

Ingredients:
- ½ red onion, chopped
- ½ pound bacon, cooked and chopped
- ½ red bell pepper, chopped
- 1 garlic clove, minced
- ½ teaspoon olive oil
- 1 sweet potato, grated
- 4 eggs, whisked
- ½ cup milk
- ½ teaspoon dill, chopped
- A pinch of red pepper, crushed
- A pinch of salt and black pepper

Directions:
In a bowl, mix eggs with onion, bacon, garlic, bell pepper, sweet potatoes, coconut milk, dill, salt, pepper and red pepper and whisk. Grease your slow cooker with the ghee, add eggs mix, cover, cook on Low for 8 hours, slice, divide between 2 plates and serve for breakfast.
Enjoy!

Nutrition: calories 261, fat 6, fiber 6, carbs 16, protein 4

Sweet Potato Casserole

Preparation time: 10 minutes
Cooking time: 6 hours
Servings: 2

Ingredients:
- 1 red onion, chopped
- 3 eggs, whisked
- 1 sweet potato, grated
- 1 tablespoon sweet paprika
- ½ pound pork, minced
- 1 teaspoon olive oil

Directions:
In a bowl, mix eggs with onions, sweet potatoes, paprika and minced meat and whisk well. Grease your slow cooker with oil, add sweet potato mix, cover, cook on Low for 6 hours, divide between 2 plates and serve for breakfast.
Enjoy!

Nutrition: calories 261, fat 7, fiber 6, carbs 16, protein 7

Breakfast Pumpkin Spread

Preparation time: 10 minutes
Cooking time: 4 hours
Servings: 2

Ingredients:
- 6 ounces pumpkin puree
- 2 tablespoons apple cider
- 2 tablespoons sugar
- ¼ teaspoon vanilla extract
- ¼ teaspoon cinnamon powder
- ½ teaspoon nutmeg, ground
- ½ teaspoon lemon juice
- ¼ teaspoon ginger, grated
- A pinch of cloves, ground
- A pinch of allspice, ground

Directions:
In your slow cooker, mix pumpkin puree with apple cider, sugar, vanilla extract, cinnamon, nutmeg, lemon juice, ginger, cloves and allspice, stir, cover and cook on Low for 4 hours. Blend using an immersion blender, cool down and serve for breakfast.
Enjoy!

Nutrition: calories 172, fat 3, fiber 3, carbs 8, protein 3

Cherry Oats

Preparation time: 10 minutes
Cooking time: 8 hours
Servings: 2

Ingredients:
- 1 cup milk
- 1 cup water
- ½ cup steel cut oats
- 1 tablespoon cocoa powder
- ¼ cup cherries, pitted
- 2 tablespoons maple syrup
- ¼ teaspoon almond extract

Directions:
In your slow cooker, combine milk with water, oats, cocoa powder, cherries, maples syrup and almond extract, stir, cover and cook on Low for 8 hours. Divide into 2 bowls and serve for breakfast.
Enjoy!

Nutrition: calories 150, fat 1, fiber 2, carbs 6, protein 5

Beans Breakfast Burrito

Preparation time: 10 minutes
Cooking time: 8 hours
Servings: 2

Ingredients:

- 6 ounces canned black beans, drained
- 1 tablespoon yellow onions, chopped
- 3 ounces feta cheese, crumbled
- 1 tablespoon green bell pepper, chopped
- ¼ teaspoon turmeric powder
- ¼ cup water
- A pinch of smoked paprika
- A pinch of cumin, ground
- A pinch of chili powder
- A pinch of salt and black pepper
- 2 whole wheat tortillas
- Salsa for serving

Directions:
In your slow cooker, mix beans with onions, cheese, bell pepper, turmeric, water, paprika, cumin, chili powder, salt and pepper, stir, cover and cook on Low for 8 hours. Divide this on each tortilla, add salsa, wrap, arrange on plates and serve for breakfast.
Enjoy!

Nutrition: calories 130, fat 4, fiber 2, carbs 5, protein 4

Mexican Rice Breakfast

Preparation time: 10 minutes
Cooking time: 2 hours
Servings: 2

Ingredients:

- ½ cup brown rice
- ½ cup onion, chopped
- 1 cup veggie stock
- ½ red bell pepper, chopped
- ½ green bell pepper, chopped
- 2 ounces canned green chilies, chopped
- 5 ounces canned black beans, drained
- A pinch of salt and black pepper
- 1 and ½ tablespoons lime juice
- ½ avocado, pitted, peeled and cubed
- 2 tablespoons cilantro, chopped
- 2 tablespoons green onions, chopped
- 2 tablespoons tomato, chopped
- ½ poblano pepper, chopped
- 1 tablespoon olive oil
- ¼ teaspoon cumin, ground

For the salsa:
Directions:
In your slow cooker, mix rice with onion, stock, red bell pepper, green bell pepper, chilies, beans, salt and pepper, stir a bit, cover and cook on High for 2 hours. Meanwhile, in a bowl, mix avocado with green onion, tomato, poblano pepper, cilantro, oil, cumin, salt, black pepper and lime juice and stir really well. Divide rice mix into 2 bowls, top each with the salsa you've just made and serve for breakfast.
Enjoy!

Nutrition: calories 140, fat 2, fiber 2, carbs 5, protein 5

Berry Butter

Preparation time: 10 minutes
Cooking time: 4 hours
Servings: 2

Ingredients:
- 1 cup blueberries puree
- ¼ teaspoon cinnamon powder
- 1 teaspoon lemon zest, grated
- 2 tablespoons sugar
- A pinch of nutmeg, ground
- A pinch of ginger, ground

Directions:
Put blueberries in your slow cooker, cover and cook on Low for 3 hours. Add sugar, ginger, nutmeg and lemon zest, stir and cook on High uncovered for 1 hour more. Divide into jars, cover and serve for breakfast cold.
Enjoy!

Nutrition: calories 143, fat 2, fiber 3, carbs 3, protein 4

Pumpkin Butter

Preparation time: 10 minutes
Cooking time: 4 hours
Servings: 2

Ingredients:
- 1 teaspoon cinnamon powder
- 1 and ½ cups pumpkin puree
- ½ cup maple syrup
- ¼ teaspoon nutmeg, ground
- ½ teaspoon vanilla extract

Directions:
In your slow cooker, mix pumpkin with maple syrup, vanilla extract, cinnamon and nutmeg, stir, cover and cook on High for 4 hours. Divide into jars and serve for breakfast!
Enjoy!

Nutrition: calories 120, fat 2, fiber 2, carbs 4, protein 2

Quinoa Pudding

Preparation time: 10 minutes
Cooking time: 8 hours
Servings: 2

Ingredients:
- 1 cup water
- ½ cup milk
- 1 tablespoon maple syrup
- ½ cup quinoa, rinsed
- ½ teaspoon vanilla extract

Directions:
In your slow cooker, mix water with milk, maple syrup, quinoa and vanilla, stir, cover and cook on Low for 8 hours. Fluff pudding with a fork, divide into 2 bowls and serve for breakfast.
Enjoy!

Nutrition: calories 120, fat 2, fiber 1, carbs 6, protein 4

Cornbread Breakfast Mix

Preparation time: 10 minutes
Cooking time: 2 hours and 30 minutes
Servings: 2

Ingredients:
- 1 garlic clove, minced
- ½ green bell pepper, chopped
- ½ yellow onion, chopped
- 5 ounces canned black beans, drained
- 5 ounces canned red kidney beans, drained
- 5 ounces canned pinto beans, drained
- 5 ounces canned tomatoes, chopped
- 3 ounces tomato sauce
- 3 ounces canned corn, drained
- 1 teaspoons chili powder
- ½ teaspoon hot sauce
- A pinch of salt and black pepper
- 2 tablespoons cornmeal
- 2 tablespoons white flour
- 1 teaspoon baking powder
- ½ tablespoon sugar
- ½ cup milk
- ½ tablespoon chia seeds
- 1 tablespoon olive oil
- Cooking spray

Directions:
Heat up a pan over medium-high heat, add garlic, bell pepper and onions, brown them for 7 minutes and transfer them to your slow cooker after you've greased it with cooking spray. Add black beans, pinto beans, red kidney beans, tomatoes, tomato sauce, corn, chili powder, salt, pepper and hot sauce to the pot, stir, cover and cook on High for 1 hour. Meanwhile, in a bowl, mix flour with cornmeal, baking powder, sugar, milk, chia seeds and the oil, stir really well, add this to the slow cooker, spread, over slow cooker again and cook on High for 1 hour and 30 minutes more. Leave cornbread to cool down, slice, divide between 2 plates and serve for breakfast.
Enjoy!

Nutrition: calories 240, fat 4, fiber 2, carbs 6, protein 9

Slow Cooker Main Dish Recipes For 2

Seafood Chowder

Preparation time: 10 minutes
Cooking time: 8 hours and 30 minutes
Servings: 2

Ingredients:
- 1 cup water
- ½ fennel bulb, chopped
- 1 sweet potato, cubed
- ½ yellow onion, chopped
- 1 bay leaf
- ½ tablespoon thyme, dried
- ½ celery rib, chopped
- Salt and black pepper to the taste
- A pinch of cayenne pepper
- ½ bottle clam juice
- 1 tablespoons white flour
- ½ cup milk
- ½ pounds salmon fillets, cubed
- 3 sea scallops, halved
- 12 shrimp, peeled and deveined
- 2 tablespoons parsley, chopped

Directions:
In your slow cooker, mix water with fennel, potatoes, onion, bay leaves, thyme, celery, clam juice, cayenne, salt and pepper, stir, cover and cook on Low for 8 hours. Add salmon, milk, scallops, flour, shrimp and parsley, toss gently, cover, cook on Low for 30 minutes more, ladle into bowls and serve.
Enjoy!

Nutrition: calories 354, fat 10, fiber 4, carbs 17, protein 12

Asian Salmon Fillets

Preparation time: 10 minutes
Cooking time: 3 hours
Servings: 2

Ingredients:
- 2 medium salmon fillets
- Salt and black pepper to the taste
- 2 tablespoons soy sauce
- 2 tablespoons maple syrup
- 16 ounces broccoli
- 2 tablespoons lemon juice
- 1 teaspoon sesame seeds

Directions:
Put broccoli florets in your slow cooker and top with salmon fillets. In a bowl, mix maple syrup with soy sauce and lemon juice, whisk really well, pour over salmon and broccoli, season with salt and black pepper to the taste, sprinkle sesame seeds on top, cover, cook on Low for 3 hours, divide everything between plates and serve.
Enjoy!

Nutrition: calories 230, fat 4, fiber 2, carbs 7, protein 6

Scallops and Shrimp Stew

Preparation time: 10 minutes
Cooking time: 3 hours and 30 minutes
Servings: 2

Ingredients:
- 1 garlic clove, minced
- 12 ounces canned tomatoes, crushed
- ½ pound sweet potatoes, peeled and cubed
- 2 cups veggie stock
- ½ small yellow onion, chopped
- ½ teaspoon cilantro, dried
- ½ teaspoon thyme, dried
- ½ teaspoon basil, dried
- A pinch of salt and black pepper
- A pinch of red pepper flakes
- A pinch of cayenne pepper
- 1 pound mixed scallops and peeled shrimp

Directions:
Put tomatoes in your slow cooker, add garlic, potatoes, stock, onion, cilantro, thyme, basil, salt, pepper, cayenne and pepper flakes, stir, cover and cook on High for 3 hours. Add scallops and shrimp, toss, cover, cook on High for 30 minutes more, divide into bowls and serve.
Enjoy!

Nutrition: calories 230, fat 3, fiber 5, carbs 17, protein 6

Spicy Tuna

Preparation time: 10 minutes
Cooking time: 4 hours and 10 minutes
Servings: 2

Ingredients:
- ½ pound tuna loin, cubed
- 1 garlic clove, minced
- 4 jalapeno peppers, chopped
- 1 cup olive oil
- 3 red chili peppers, chopped
- 2 teaspoons black peppercorns, ground
- A pinch of sea salt
- Black pepper to the taste

Directions:
Put the oil in your slow cooker, add chili peppers, jalapenos, peppercorns, salt, pepper and garlic, whisk, cover and cook on Low for 4 hours. Add tuna, toss, cook on High for 10 minutes, divide between plates and serve.
Enjoy!

Nutrition: calories 200, fat 4, fiber 6, carbs 16, protein 4

Simple Flavored Salmon

Preparation time: 10 minutes
Cooking time: 2 hours
Servings: 2

Ingredients:
- 2 medium salmon fillets, boneless
- A pinch of nutmeg, ground
- A pinch of cloves, ground
- A pinch of ginger powder
- A pinch of salt and black pepper
- 2 teaspoons sugar
- 1 teaspoon onion powder
- ¼ teaspoon chipotle chili powder
- ½ teaspoon cayenne pepper
- ½ teaspoon cinnamon, ground

Directions:
In a bowl, mix salmon fillets with nutmeg, cloves, ginger, salt, coconut sugar, onion powder, chili powder, cayenne black pepper and cinnamon, toss, divide fish into 2 tin foil pieces, wrap, place in your slow cooker, cover, cook on Low for 2 hours. unwrap fish, divide between plates and serve.
Enjoy!

Nutrition: calories 220, fat 13, fiber 6, carbs 16, protein 4

Coconut Clams

Preparation time: 10 minutes
Cooking time: 6 hours
Servings: 2

Ingredients:
- 10 ounces canned clams, chopped
- ¼ cup coconut milk
- 2 eggs, whisked
- 1 tablespoon olive oil
- 1 green bell pepper, chopped
- 1 yellow onion, chopped
- A pinch of salt and black pepper

Directions:
Put clams in your slow cooker, add milk, eggs, oil, onion, bell pepper, salt and black pepper, stir, cover and cook on Low for 6 hours. Divide into bowls and serve right away.
Enjoy!

Nutrition: calories 270, fat 4, fiber 7, carbs 13, protein 7

Clam Chowder

Preparation time: 10 minutes
Cooking time: 3 hours and 30 minutes
Servings: 2

Ingredients:
- 2 bacon slices, cooked and chopped
- 1 small yellow onion, chopped
- 1 carrot, chopped
- 6 ounces canned clams, chopped
- 1 sweet potato, chopped
- 1 cup water
- 1 teaspoon Worcestershire sauce
- 2 tablespoons flour
- 12 ounces coconut milk

Directions:
In your slow cooker, mix water with clams, carrot, onion, bacon, potato and Worcestershire sauce, stir, cover and cook on High for 3 hours. Add coconut milk mixed with flour, stir, cook on High for 30 minutes more, divide chowder into bowls and serve.
Enjoy!

Nutrition: calories 230, fat 10, fiber 7, carbs 18, protein 10

Pulled Chicken

Preparation time: 10 minutes
Cooking time: 6 hours
Servings: 2

Ingredients:
- 2 tomatoes, chopped
- 2 red onions, chopped
- 2 chicken breasts, skinless and boneless
- 2 garlic cloves, minced
- 1 tablespoon maple syrup
- 1 teaspoon chili powder
- 1 teaspoon basil, dried
- 3 tablespoons water
- 1 teaspoon cloves

Directions:
In your slow cooker mix onion with tomatoes, chicken, garlic, maple syrup, chili powder, basil, water and cloves, toss well, cover and cook on Low for 6 hours. Shred chicken, divide it along with the veggies between plates, and serve right away!
Enjoy!

Nutrition: calories 200, fat 3, fiber 3, carbs 17, protein 6

Chicken Chili

Preparation time: 10 minutes
Cooking time: 7 hours
Servings: 2

Ingredients:
- 7 ounces jarred salsa
- 4 chicken thighs
- 1 small yellow onion, chopped
- 7 ounces canned tomatoes, chopped
- 1 red bell pepper, chopped
- 1 tablespoon chili powder

Directions:
1. Put the salsa in your slow cooker, add chicken, onion, tomatoes, bell pepper and chili powder, stir, cover, cook on Low for 7 hours, divide chili into bowls and serve.

Enjoy!

Nutrition: calories 240, fat 3, fiber 7, carbs 17, protein 8

Chicken and Mushrooms

Preparation time: 10 minutes
Cooking time: 6 hours
Servings: 2

Ingredients:
- 2 tablespoons tomato paste
- 1 onion, chopped
- 1 tablespoon olive oil
- 1 teaspoon oregano, dried
- 1 garlic clove, minced
- A pinch of red pepper flakes
- 1 pound mushrooms, sliced
- ¼ cup chicken stock
- 4 ounces canned tomatoes, chopped
- 4 chicken thighs
- A pinch of salt and black pepper to the taste

Directions:
Heat up a pan with the oil over medium-high heat, add onion and garlic, stir, cook for 2 minutes and transfer this to your slow cooker. Add tomato paste, oregano, pepper flakes, mushrooms, tomatoes, stock, chicken pieces, salt and black pepper, stir well, cover and cook on Low for 6 hours. Divide into bowls and serve.
Enjoy!

Nutrition: calories 240, fat 4, fiber 6, carbs 18, protein 10

Indian Chicken

Preparation time: 10 minutes
Cooking time: 6 hours
Servings: 2

Ingredients:
- 1 cup tomato puree
- 2 tablespoons cashews, chopped
- 2 tablespoons water
- 1 pound chicken thighs, skinless, boneless and cubed
- 1 tablespoons garam masala
- 1 garlic clove, minced
- ½ small yellow onion, chopped
- ½ teaspoon ginger powder
- A pinch of salt and cayenne pepper
- ½ teaspoon sweet paprika
- 2 tablespoons cilantro, chopped

Directions:
Put the tomato puree in your slow cooker, add chicken pieces, garlic, garam masala, onion, ginger powder, salt, cayenne pepper and paprika, stir, cover and cook on Low for 6 hours. In your blender, mix cashews with the water, pulse really well, add this to your chicken, stir well, divide into bowls and sprinkle cilantro on top.
Enjoy!

Nutrition: calories 259, fat 3, fiber 7, carbs 17, protein 14

Turkey with Cherries, Cranberries and Figs

Preparation time: 10 minutes
Cooking time: 8 hours
Servings: 2

Ingredients:
- 1 pound turkey breast, bone in
- ½ cup black figs
- 1 sweet potato, cut into wedges
- ¼ cup dried cherries, pitted
- 1 white onion, cut into wedges
- ¼ cup dried cranberries
- ¼ cup water
- ½ teaspoon onion powder
- ¼ teaspoon garlic powder
- ½ teaspoon parsley flakes
- ½ teaspoon thyme, dried
- ¼ teaspoon sage, dried
- ½ teaspoon paprika, dried
- A pinch of salt and black pepper to the taste

Directions:
Put the turkey breast in your slow cooker, add sweet potato, figs, cherries, onions, cranberries, water, parsley, garlic, onion powder, thyme, sage, paprika, salt and pepper, stir, cover and cook on Low for 8 hours. Discard bone from turkey breast, slice meat, divide between plates and serve with the veggies, figs, cherries and berries on the side.
Enjoy!

Nutrition: calories 220, fat 5, fiber 8, carbs 18, protein 15

Turkey and Sweet Potatoes

Preparation time: 10 minutes
Cooking time: 8 hours
Servings: 2

Ingredients:
- 1 pound turkey breast, skinless and boneless
- ½ cup cranberries, chopped
- 1 sweet potato, chopped
- 2 tablespoons raisins
- 2 tablespoons walnuts, chopped
- ½ sweet onion, chopped
- 1 tablespoon lemon juice
- ½ cup sugar
- ½ teaspoon ginger, grated
- ¼ teaspoon nutmeg, ground
- ½ teaspoon cinnamon powder
- ¼ cup veggie stock
- Salt and black pepper to the taste
- ½ teaspoon poultry seasoning
- 3 tablespoons olive oil

Directions:
Heat up a pan with the oil over medium-high heat, add cranberries, walnuts, raisins, onion, lemon juice, sugar, ginger, nutmeg, cinnamon, stock and black pepper, stir well, bring to a simmer and take off heat. Place turkey breast in your slow cooker, add sweet potatoes, cranberries mix and poultry seasoning, toss a bit, cover and cook on Low for 8 hours. Slice turkey breast and divide between plates, add sweet potatoes, drizzle the sauce from the cooker all over and serve.
Enjoy!

Nutrition: calories 264, fat 4, fiber 6, carbs 15, protein 15

Slow Cooked Chicken

Preparation time: 10 minutes
Cooking time: 6 hours
Servings: 2

Ingredients:
- ½ chicken, cut into medium pieces
- 2 thyme sprigs, chopped
- 1 celery stalk, chopped
- 1 garlic clove, minced
- 1 carrot, chopped
- ½ yellow onion, chopped
- A pinch of salt and white pepper
- Juice of ½ lemon

Directions:
Put thyme, garlic, celery, onion and carrots in your slow cooker, add chicken on top, season salt and white pepper, drizzle the lemon juice, cover and cook on Low for 6 hours. Divide chicken on plates and serve with cooking juices drizzled all over.
Enjoy!

Nutrition: calories 320, fat 4, fiber 7, carbs 16, protein 6

Roasted Beef Chuck

Preparation time: 10 minutes
Cooking time: 8 hours and 30 minutes
Servings: 2

Ingredients:
- 2 pounds beef chuck roast
- ½ cup veggie stock
- ½ tablespoon olive oil
- 1 bay leaf
- 5 thyme springs
- 2 garlic cloves, minced
- ½ carrot, roughly chopped
- 1 celery rib, roughly chopped
- ¼ cauliflower head, florets separated
- A pinch of salt and black pepper to the taste
- 1 small yellow onion, roughly chopped

Directions:
Heat up a pan with the oil over medium-high heat, add beef roast, season with salt and pepper, brown for 5 minutes on each side and then transfer to your slow cooker. Add thyme, stock, bay leaf, garlic, celery, onion and carrot, cover and cook on Low for 8 hours. Add cauliflower, cook on High for 20 minutes more, slice roast, divide it and veggies between plates and serve. Enjoy!

Nutrition: calories 340, fat 5, fiber 7, carbs 18, protein 22

Pork Chops and Pineapple Mix

Preparation time: 10 minutes
Cooking time: 6 hours
Servings: 2

Ingredients:
- 1 pound pork chops
- 2 tablespoons sugar
- 2 tablespoons ketchup
- 6 ounces pineapple, cubed
- 1 tablespoon apple cider vinegar
- 2 tablespoons soy sauce
- 1 teaspoon garlic, minced
- 1 tablespoon white flour
- 1 tablespoon cilantro, chopped

Directions:
In a bowl, mix ketchup with sugar, vinegar, soy sauce and flour and whisk well. Add pork chops, toss well, transfer everything to your slow cooker, add pineapple and garlic, toss again, cover and cook on Low for 6 hours. Sprinkle cilantro, divide everything between plates and serve. Enjoy!

Nutrition: calories 345, fat 5, fiber 7, carbs 17, protein 14

Pork and Apples

Preparation time: 10 minutes
Cooking time: 8 hours
Servings: 2

Ingredients:
- A pinch of nutmeg, ground
- 1 pound pork tenderloin
- 2 apples, cored and sliced
- 1 tablespoon maple syrup

Directions:
Place apples in your slow cooker, sprinkle nutmeg all over, add pork tenderloin, sprinkle some more nutmeg and drizzle the maple syrup. Cover, cook on Low for 8 hours, slice pork tenderloin, divide it between plates and serve with apple slices and cooking juices on top.
Enjoy!

Nutrition: calories 400, fat 12, fiber 8, carbs 18, protein 20

Lamb Stew

Preparation time: 10 minutes
Cooking time: 8 hours
Servings: 2

Ingredients:
- 1 pound lamb meat, cubed
- 2 tablespoons flour
- Salt and black pepper to the taste
- 1 tablespoon olive oil
- ½ teaspoon rosemary, dried
- 1 small onion, sliced
- ¼ teaspoon thyme, dried
- 1 cup water
- ½ cup baby carrots
- 1 cup sweet potatoes, chopped

Directions:
In a bowl, mix lamb with flour and toss to coat. Heat up a pan with the oil over medium-high heat, add meat, brown it on all sides and transfer to your slow cooker. Add onion, salt, pepper, rosemary, thyme, water, carrots and sweet potatoes, stir, cover and cook on Low for 8 hours. Divide lamb stew between plates and serve hot.
Enjoy!

Nutrition: calories 350, fat 8, fiber 3, carbs 14, protein 16

Pork Roast and Veggies

Preparation time: 10 minutes
Cooking time: 4 hours
Servings: 2

Ingredients:
- ½ pound sweet potatoes, chopped
- 1 pound pork roast
- 2 medium carrots, chopped
- 6 ounces canned tomatoes, chopped
- 1 small yellow onion, chopped
- Grated zest and juice of ½ lemon
- 2 garlic cloves, minced
- 1 bay leaf
- Salt and black pepper to the taste
- 2 tablespoons kalamata olives, pitted and chopped

Directions:
Put potatoes in your slow cooker, add carrots, tomatoes, onions, lemon juice, lemon zest, pork, bay leaf, salt, black pepper and garlic, stir, cover and cook on High for 4 hours. Transfer meat to a cutting board, slice and divide it between plates. Add veggies and olives next to the meat and serve right away!
Enjoy!

Nutrition: calories 360, fat 4, fiber 3, carbs 17, protein 27

Beef Stew

Preparation time: 10 minutes
Cooking time: 4 hours and 10 minutes
Servings: 2

Ingredients:
- 1 tablespoon olive oil
- 4 ounces mushrooms, sliced
- ½ yellow onion, chopped
- 1 pound beef meat, cubed
- ½ cup veggie stock
- 6 ounces canned tomatoes, chopped
- 2 tablespoons tomato sauce
- 2 tablespoons balsamic vinegar
- 2 tablespoons garlic cloves, minced
- 2 ounces black olives, pitted and sliced
- 1 tablespoon rosemary, chopped
- 1 tablespoon parsley, chopped
- ½ tablespoon capers
- Salt and black pepper to the taste

Directions:
Heat up a pan with the oil over medium-high heat, add beef, cook for 3-4 minutes and transfer them to your slow cooker. Add onion, mushrooms, stock, tomatoes, tomato sauce, vinegar, garlic, olives, parsley, capers, salt, black pepper and rosemary, stir gently, cover and cook on High for 4 hours. Divide between plates and serve right away!
Enjoy!

Nutrition: calories 370, fat 14, fiber 6, carbs 26, protein 38

Slow Cooked Beef Stew and Red Wine

Preparation time: 10 minutes
Cooking time: 8 hours
Servings: 2

Ingredients:
- ½ cup beef stock
- 1 tablespoon white flour
- ½ teaspoon mustard
- 2 carrots, chopped
- 2 ounces cremini mushrooms, halved
- ½ red onion, roughly chopped
- 1 celery rib, chopped
- 1 garlic clove, minced
- 2 thyme springs
- ½ tablespoon olive oil
- 1 pound beef roast, cut into medium cubes
- Salt and black pepper to the taste
- 2 tablespoons tomato paste
- ¼ cup red wine
- ½ tablespoon butter
- 1 tablespoon parsley, chopped

Directions:
Put the stock in your slow cooker, add mustard and flour and whisk well. Add carrots, mushrooms, onion, garlic, thyme, celery, and stir. Heat up a pan with the oil over medium-high heat, add beef meat, brown for a few minutes on each side and transfer it to your slow cooker. Add salt, pepper, tomato paste, butter and wine, stir, cover and cook on Low for 8 hours. Discard thyme, divide stew into bowls, and sprinkle parsley on top and serve.
Enjoy!

Nutrition: calories 433, fat 20, fiber 4, carbs 14, protein 39

Slow Cooked Pasta Dish

Preparation time: 10 minutes
Cooking time: 6 hours and 30 minutes
Servings: 2

Ingredients:
- ½ pound beef sausage, ground
- ½ teaspoon garlic, minced
- ½ red onion, chopped
- Salt and black pepper to the taste
- ½ teaspoon basil, dried
- ½ teaspoon parsley, dried
- 14 ounces canned tomatoes, chopped
- 1 cup pasta sauce
- 1 and ½ cups chicken stock
- 2 cups short pasta
- ½ cup mozzarella, shredded

Directions:
Heat up a pan over medium-high heat, add onion, garlic and meat, stir brown for a few minutes and transfer to your slow cooker. Add salt, pepper, basil, parsley, tomatoes, pasta sauce and stock, stir, cover and cook on Low for 6 hours. Add pasta, stir, cover and cook on Low for 30 minutes more. Add mozzarella, leave aside for a few minutes until cheese melts, divide everything between plates and serve.
Enjoy!

Nutrition: calories 300, fat 6, fiber 8, carbs 18, protein 17

Honey Roast

Preparation time: 10 minutes
Cooking time: 6 hours
Servings: 2

Ingredients:
- 1 pound pork loin roast, boneless
- 3 tablespoons honey
- ½ cup parmesan, grated
- 1 tablespoon soy sauce
- ½ tablespoon basil, dried
- ½ tablespoons oregano, dried
- 1 tablespoon garlic, minced
- 1 tablespoons olive oil
- Salt and black pepper to the taste
- 1 tablespoon cornstarch
- 2 tablespoons chicken stock

Directions:
In your slow cooker, mix pork loin roast with honey, soy sauce, parmesan, basil, oregano, garlic, oil, salt and pepper, toss well, cover and cook on Low for 6 hours. In a small pot, mix cornstarch with stock, stir well and bring to a simmer over medium heat. Transfer roast to a cutting board, shred and divide between plates. Add stock mix to your slow cooker, stir well and pour over roast. Serve right away.
Enjoy!

Nutrition: calories 374, fat 6, fiber 8, carbs 29, protein 6

Creamy Beef Mix

Preparation time: 10 minutes
Cooking time: 8 hours
Servings: 2

Ingredients:
- 1 pound beef stew meat
- 1 teaspoon Italian seasoning
- Salt and black pepper to the taste
- 1 cup beef stock
- ½ cup mushrooms, sliced
- 1 and ½ tablespoon Worcestershire sauce
- 1 teaspoon garlic, minced
- ½ tablespoon mustard
- ½ cup sour cream
- 2 ounces cream cheese, soft
- 2 tablespoons cornstarch
- 6 ounces pasta noodles, cooked
- Cooking spray

Directions:
Grease your slow cooker with cooking spray, add meat, salt, pepper, Italian seasoning, stock, mushrooms, Worcestershire sauce, garlic and mustard, stir, cover and cook on Low for 7 hours and 30 minutes. Add cornstarch, sour cream and cream cheese, stir, cover and cook on Low for 30 minutes more. Divide pasta on plates, top each with beef mix and serve.
Enjoy!

Nutrition: calories 372, fat 6, fiber 9, carbs 18, protein 22

Turkey and Chickpeas Stew

Preparation time: 10 minutes
Cooking time: 8 hours and 10 minutes
Servings: 2

Ingredients:
- ½ pound turkey, ground
- Cooking spray
- ½ tablespoon olive oil
- 1 small yellow onion, chopped
- 1 garlic clove, minced
- 1 tablespoon poblano pepper, chopped
- ¼ cup celery, chopped
- ¼ cup carrots, chopped
- 6 ounces canned tomatoes, chopped
- 6 ounces canned chickpeas, drained
- ½ cup chicken stock
- ½ teaspoon turmeric powder
- ½ teaspoon sweet paprika
- 1 bay leaf
- ½ teaspoon coriander, ground
- A pinch of red pepper flakes
- ½ tablespoon parsley, chopped
- Salt and black pepper to the taste

Directions:
Heat up a pan with the olive oil over medium-high heat, add turkey, onion and garlic, stir, brown for 10 minutes and take off heat. Grease your slow cooker with cooking spray and add turkey mix. Also add, poblano, celery, carrots, tomatoes, chickpeas, stock, turmeric, paprika, bay leaf, coriander, pepper flakes, parsley, salt and pepper, stir, cover and cook on Low for 8 hours. Divide into bowls and serve.
Enjoy!

Nutrition: calories 462, fat 7, fiber 9, carbs 30, protein 17

Lentils Soup

Preparation time: 10 minutes
Cooking time: 4 hours
Servings: 2

Ingredients:
- 2 garlic cloves, minced
- 1 carrot, chopped
- ½ white onion, chopped
- 3 cups chicken stock
- ½ cup brown lentils, rinsed
- ½ tablespoon curry powder
- ½ teaspoon garam masala
- ½ teaspoon cumin, ground
- 1 bay leaf
- 1 cup baby spinach
- 1 and ½ tablespoon lemon juice
- 1 tablespoon cilantro, chopped
- Salt and black pepper to the taste

Directions:
In your slow cooker, mix garlic with carrot, onion, stock, lentils, curry powder, garam masala, cumin, bay leaf, baby spinach, salt and pepper, stir, cover and cook on High for 4 hours. Add lemon juice and cilantro, stir, ladle into bowls and serve.
Enjoy!

Nutrition: calories 361, fat 7, fiber 7, carbs 16, protein 5

Slow Cooked Chicken Mix

Preparation time: 10 minutes
Cooking time: 4 hours
Servings: 2

Ingredients:
- ½ pound rotisserie chicken, shredded
- 6 ounces great northern beans, drained
- 1 garlic clove, minced
- ½ celery stalk, chopped
- 1 bay leaf
- 1 small yellow onion, chopped
- ½ cup chicken stock
- ¼ cup apple cider
- ½ teaspoon thyme, chopped
- ½ teaspoon sage, chopped
- ¼ teaspoon chili powder
- ¼ teaspoon sweet paprika
- A pinch of salt and black pepper
- A pinch of cayenne pepper

Directions:
In your slow cooker, mix chicken with beans, garlic, celery, bay leaf, onion, stock, apple cider, thyme, sage, chili powder, paprika, salt, pepper and cayenne, stir, cover and cook on High for 4 hours. Divide into bowls and serve right away.
Enjoy!

Nutrition: calories 351, fat 6, fiber 7, carbs 17, protein 16

Lemon Chicken

Preparation time: 10 minutes
Cooking time: 4 hours
Servings: 2

Ingredients:
- 1 pound red potatoes, cut into quarters
- 2 chicken thighs, bone in
- 1 small yellow onion, cut into wedges
- 2 tablespoons olive oil
- 1 and ½ tablespoon lemon juice
- 2 garlic cloves, minced
- 1 rosemary spring, chopped
- 3 thyme sprigs, chopped
- Salt and black pepper to the taste

Directions:
In your slow cooker, mix potatoes with chicken thighs, onion, olive oil, lemon juice, garlic, rosemary, thyme, salt and pepper, stir, cover and cook on High for 4 hours. Divide between plates and serve right away.
Enjoy!

Nutrition: calories 324, fat 7, fiber 8, carbs 20, protein 17

Tasty Gumbo

Preparation time: 10 minutes
Cooking time: 6 hours
Servings: 2
Ingredients:

- ½ pound chicken breast, skinless, boneless and cubed
- ½ pound smoked sausage, sliced
- ½ pound shrimp, peeled and deveined
- ½ yellow onion, chopped
- ½ green bell pepper, chopped
- ½ jalapeno, chopped
- Salt and black pepper to the taste
- 1 celery rib, chopped
- 12 ounces canned tomatoes, chopped
- 1 and ½ teaspoon garlic, minced
- 1 cup chicken stock
- ½ tablespoon Cajun seasoning
- ½ teaspoon thyme, dried
- ½ teaspoon oregano, dried

Directions:
In your slow cooker, mix chicken with sausage, onion, bell pepper, jalapeno, celery, salt, pepper, tomatoes, garlic, stock, Cajun seasoning, thyme and oregano, stir, cover and cook on Low for 5 hours and 30 minutes. Add shrimp, toss, cover, and cook on Low for 30 minutes more, divide into bowls and serve.
Enjoy!

Nutrition: calories 361, fat 6, fiber 8, carbs 14, protein 5

Chicken Soup

Preparation time: 10 minutes
Cooking time: 8 hours
Servings: 2
Ingredients:

- ½ pound chicken thighs, skinless and bone in
- ½ small yellow onion, chopped
- ½ red bell pepper, chopped
- 1 garlic clove, minced
- 1 cup chicken stock
- 6 ounces canned tomatoes, chopped
- 4 ounces canned tomato sauce
- 2 ounces canned green chilies, chopped
- ½ teaspoon oregano, dried
- ½ teaspoon chili powder
- A pinch of cumin, ground
- A pinch of salt and black pepper
- 1 yellow squash, halved and chopped
- 1 ounce green beans, halved
- ½ tablespoon lime juice
- 1 tablespoon cilantro, chopped

Directions:
In your slow cooker, mix chicken with onion, bell pepper, garlic, stock, tomatoes, tomato sauce, green chilies, oregano, chili powder, cumin, salt and pepper, stir, cover and cook on Low for 7 hours and 30 minutes. Add squash, green beans, limejuice and cilantro, stir, cover and cook on Low for 30 minutes more. Ladle soup into bowls and serve.
Enjoy!

Nutrition: calories 254, fat 6, fiber 6, carbs 18, protein 22

Italian Pork Loin

Preparation time: 10 minutes
Cooking time: 4 hours
Servings: 2

Ingredients:

- 6 ounces canned cannellini beans, drained
- 1 small red bell pepper, chopped
- ¼ cup yellow onion, chopped
- 1 teaspoon Italian seasoning
- ½ tablespoon olive oil
- ½ pound pork loin, boneless
- Salt and black pepper to the taste
- 1 ounce mozzarella cheese, shredded
- 6 ounces canned roasted tomatoes, drained and chopped
- 1 tablespoon basil, chopped

Directions:
Put the oil in your slow cooker, add pork loin, beans, red bell pepper, onion, Italian seasoning, salt, pepper, tomatoes and basil, stir, cover and cook on Low for 4 hours. Add cheese, leave aside until it melts, divide between plates and serve.
Enjoy!

Nutrition: calories 385, fat 12, fiber 5, carbs 18, protein 40

Spinach and Mushroom Tortellini

Preparation time: 10 minutes
Cooking time: 7 hours
Servings: 2

Ingredients:

- 4 ounces white mushrooms, sliced
- ½ cup yellow onion, chopped
- 2 tablespoons butter, melted
- 1 tablespoon soy sauce
- Salt and black pepper to the taste
- 1 cup veggie stock
- 10 ounces cheese filled tortellini
- 3 ounces cream cheese, soft and cubed
- 1 and ½ cups baby spinach leaves
- 2 tablespoons parmesan, grated
- 1 tablespoon basil, chopped

Directions:
In your slow cooker, mix butter with mushrooms, onions, soy sauce, salt, pepper and stock, stir, cover and cook on Low for 6 hours and 45 minutes. Add cream cheese and tortellini, toss, cover and cook on Low for 15 minutes more. Add spinach and parmesan, stir, leave aside for a few minutes until cheese melts, divide between plates and serve.
Enjoy!

Nutrition: calories 400, fat 15, fiber 4, carbs 25, protein 14

Bacon Chili

Preparation time: 10 minutes
Cooking time: 3 hours
Servings: 2

Ingredients:
- ½ pound bacon, chopped
- ½ pound beef, ground
- ½ red bell pepper, chopped
- 1 garlic clove, minced
- ½ cup yellow onion, chopped
- 10 ounces canned roasted tomatoes, crushed
- 7 ounces canned red kidney beans, drained
- 2 ounces canned green chilies, chopped
- ½ cup corn
- Salt and black pepper to the taste
- 1 tablespoon chili powder

Directions:
Heat up a pan over medium-high heat, add bacon, stir, cook for 10 minutes and transfer to your slow cooker. Heat up the pan again over medium-high heat, add beef, brown for a few minutes and transfer to your slow cooker as well. Add bell pepper, garlic, onion, tomatoes, beans, chilies, corn, salt, pepper and chili powder, stir, cover and cook on High for 3 hours. Divide into bowls and serve right away.
Enjoy!

Nutrition: calories 400, fat 14, fiber 5, carbs 29, protein 22

French Chicken Dish

Preparation time: 10 minutes
Cooking time: 4 hours
Servings: 2

Ingredients:
- 2 tablespoons butter, melted
- Salt and black pepper to the taste
- 4 cups sweet onions, chopped
- ¼ cup chicken stock
- 1 tablespoon water
- 2 chicken breast halves, bone in and skin on
- 1 tablespoon cornstarch
- 1 tablespoon parsley, chopped
- Cooking spray

Directions:
Heat up a pan with the butter over medium-high heat, add onions, thyme, salt and pepper, stir and cook for 15 minutes. Reduce heat to medium, cook onions for 10 minutes more, add stock, stir and take off heat. Grease your slow cooker with cooking spray, add chicken, onions mix, water mixed with cornstarch, salt and pepper, stir, cover and cook on High for 4 hours. Add parsley, stir, divide between plates and serve.
Enjoy!

Nutrition: calories 453, fat 15, fiber 5, carbs 20, protein 20

BBQ Short Ribs

Preparation time: 10 minutes
Cooking time: 8 hours
Servings: 2

Ingredients:

- 2 beef short ribs, bone in and cut into individual ribs
- Salt and black pepper to the taste
- ¼ cup beef stock
- ½ cup BBQ sauce
- 1 tablespoon mustard
- 1 tablespoon green onions, chopped

Directions:
In your slow cooker, mix ribs with salt, pepper, stock, BBQ sauce and mustard, toss well, cover and cook on Low for 8 hours. Add green onions, toss, divide between plates and serve.
Enjoy!

Nutrition: calories 284, fat 7, 4, carbs 18, protein 20

Smooth Beef Brisket

Preparation time: 10 minutes
Cooking time: 8 hours and 20 minutes
Servings: 2

Ingredients:

- 1 and ½ tablespoon olive oil
- 1 shallot, chopped
- 3 ounces baby mushrooms, sliced
- 1 teaspoon garlic, minced
- 1 pound beef brisket
- Salt and black pepper to the taste
- ¼ cup beef stock
- 1 tablespoon soy sauce
- 2 teaspoons Worcestershire sauce
- ½ tablespoon cornstarch
- 3 tablespoons heavy cream
- 1 tablespoon parsley, chopped

Directions:
Heat up a pan with the oil over medium-high heat, add shallot, garlic and mushrooms, stir, cook for 4-5 minutes and transfer to your slow cooker. Heat up the pan again over medium-high heat, add beef, brown for 3 minutes on each side and transfer to your slow cooker. Add stock, soy sauce, Worcestershire sauce, salt and pepper, stir, cover and cook on Low for 8 hours. Transfer beef to a cutting board, slice and divide between plates. Transfer cooking juices from the slow cooker to a pan, heat up over medium heat, add cornstarch, cream and parsley, stir well, cook for a couple of minutes, drizzle over beef and serve.
Enjoy!

Nutrition: calories 400, fat 10, fiber 4, carbs 15, protein 20

White Chicken Soup

Preparation time: 10 minutes
Cooking time: 4 hours and 30 minutes
Servings: 2

Ingredients:
- ½ pound chicken breasts, skinless and boneless
- 1 tablespoon butter
- 1 small yellow onion, chopped
- 1 carrot, chopped
- 1 small red bell pepper, chopped
- ½ cup mushrooms, sliced
- 1 garlic clove, minced
- ½ teaspoon Italian seasoning
- Salt and black pepper to the taste
- 3 cups chicken stock
- ½ cup half and half
- 1 tablespoon cornstarch
- 4 lasagna noodles, broken
- 4 ounces canned navy beans, drained
- 1 cup baby spinach
- 1 ounce parmesan, grated
- 1 ounce mozzarella cheese, shredded

Directions:
In your slow cooker, mix chicken with butter, onion, carrot, bell pepper, mushrooms, garlic, Italian seasoning, salt, pepper, navy beans and stock, stir, cover and cook on High for 4 hours. In a bowl, mix cornstarch with half-and-half and stir well. Add this mix to your slow cooker, also add lasagna noodles and baby spinach, stir, cover and cook on High for 30 minutes. Add parmesan and mozzarella, stir, leave aside for a few minutes, divide into bowls and serve.
Enjoy!

Nutrition: calories 453, fat 14, fiber 6, carbs 28, protein 33

Potato and Bacon Soup

Preparation time: 10 minutes
Cooking time: 5 hours and 15 minutes
Servings: 2

Ingredients:
- 2 bacon slices, chopped
- 1 small yellow onion, chopped
- 2 cups chicken stock
- 1 gold potato, cubed
- 1 ounce ranch seasoning
- ½ cup heavy whipping cream
- 1 tablespoon cornstarch
- 1 tablespoon water
- 2 ounces cream cheese, cubed
- 2 ounces cheddar cheese, grated

Directions:
In your slow cooker, mix bacon with onion, stock, potato and ranch seasoning, stir, cover and cook on Low for 5 hours. In a bowl, mix cornstarch with water, stir well and add to your slow cooker. Also, add heavy cream, cream cheese and cheddar, stir, cook on High for 15 minutes more, divide into bowls and serve.
Enjoy!

Nutrition: calories 372, fat 15, fiber 4, carbs 20, protein 22

Delicious Chicken and Rice

Preparation time: 10 minutes
Cooking time: 2 hours and 25 minutes
Servings: 2

Ingredients:
- 1 teaspoon chicken taco seasoning
- Salt and black pepper to the taste
- ¼ teaspoon cumin, ground
- 2 chicken thighs, skinless and boneless
- 3 ounces canned roasted tomatoes, chopped
- 3 ounces canned black beans, drained
- ¼ cup corn
- 2 ounces cream cheese, cubed
- 2 ounces cheddar cheese
- 1 and ½ cups white rice, already cooked
- 2 tablespoons cilantro, chopped

Directions:
In your slow cooker, mix chicken with salt, pepper, cumin, taco seasoning, tomatoes, beans and corn, stir, cover and cook on High for 2 hours. Transfer chicken to a cutting board, shred using 2 forks, return to slow cooker and mix with rice, cheddar and cream cheese. Toss everything, cover, cook on High for 25 minutes more, divide between plates and serve with cilantro sprinkled on top.
Enjoy!

Nutrition: calories 372, fat 12, fiber 5, carbs 20, protein 25

Mixed Pork, Beef and Beans

Preparation time: 10 minutes
Cooking time: 8 hours
Servings: 2

Ingredients:
- ½ pound black beans
- 1 bacon slice, chopped
- ½ pound pork shoulder, cubed
- Salt and black pepper to the taste
- ½ pound beef chuck, boneless and cut into medium cubes
- 3 garlic cloves, minced
- ½ yellow onion, chopped
- ½ cup chicken stock
- ¼ pound smoked ham hock
- ¼ tablespoon apple cider vinegar
- ½ bunch collard greens
- 1 tablespoon olive oil

Directions:
In your slow cooker, mix beans with bacon, pork, salt, pepper, beef, 2 garlic cloves, onion, stock and apple cider, stir, cover, cook on Low for 8 hours and divide everything between plates. Heat up a pan with the oil over medium-high heat, add the rest of the garlic, stir and cook for 1 minute. Add collard greens, stir, cook for a few minutes and divide next to meat and beans. Serve right away.
Enjoy!

Nutrition: calories 453, fat 10, fiber 12, carbs 20, protein 36

Pork Chops and Creamy Sauce

Preparation time: 10 minutes
Cooking time: 4 hours
Servings: 2

Ingredients:
- ½ pound pork loin chops
- 1 small yellow onion, chopped
- ¼ tablespoon butter
- ¼ tablespoons olive oil
- 1 garlic clove, minced
- ¼ teaspoon thyme, dried
- Salt and black pepper to the taste
- ¼ teaspoon mustard powder
- ½ cup chicken stock
- ¼ cup heavy cream
- ¼ tablespoon cornstarch
- ½ teaspoon parsley, dried
- ½ teaspoon basil, dried

Directions:
Grease your slow cooker with the oil and the butter, add pork chops, onion, garlic, thyme, salt, pepper, mustard powder, stock, parsley and basil, stir, cover and cook on High for 4 hours. In a bowl, mix heavy cream with cornstarch, add to the pot, cover, cook for 15 minutes more, divide everything between plates and serve.
Enjoy!

Nutrition: calories 453, fat 16, fiber 8, carbs 7, protein 27

Balsamic Chicken Mix

Preparation time: 10 minutes
Cooking time: 6 hours
Servings: 2

Ingredients:
- 1 pound chicken breast, skinless and boneless
- ½ tablespoon honey
- 2 tablespoons peach preserves
- 1 tablespoon balsamic vinegar
- ½ teaspoon garlic, minced
- 1 cup farro, already cooked
- 1 peach, pitted and slices
- ½ cup blueberries
- ¼ cup cherry tomatoes, halved
- 1 tablespoon basil, chopped

Directions:
In your slow cooker, mix chicken with honey, peach preserves, vinegar and garlic, stir, cover and cook on Low for 6 hours. Shred meat using 2 forks and divide into 2 bowls. In addition, divide farro, peach slices, blueberries and cherry tomatoes between the 2 bowls, drizzle some of the cooking juices from the pan all over, sprinkle basil on top and serve.
Enjoy!

Nutrition: calories 300, fat 7, fiber 8, carbs 20, protein 39

Chicken Drumsticks and Blue Cheese Sauce

Preparation time: 10 minutes
Cooking time: 8 hours
Servings: 2

Ingredients:
- 1 pound chicken drumsticks
- 2 tablespoons buffalo wing sauce
- 2 tablespoons apricot preserves
- 2 tablespoons BBQ sauce
- 2 tablespoons honey
- 2 tablespoons blue cheese, crumbled
- 2 tablespoons sour cream
- 2 tablespoons milk
- 1 teaspoon lemon juice
- Salt and black pepper to the taste

For the sauce:

Directions:
In your slow cooker, mix chicken pieces with wing sauce, apricot preserves, BBQ sauce and honey, stir, cover and cook on Low for 8 hours. In a bowl, mix blue cheese with sour cream, milk, lemon juice, salt and pepper and whisk really well. Divide chicken drumsticks on plates, drizzle blue cheese sauce all over them and serve.
Enjoy!

Nutrition: calories 361, fat 7, fiber 8, carbs 18, protein 22

Mustard Pork Chops

Preparation time: 10 minutes
Cooking time: 4 hours
Servings: 2

Ingredients:
- 1 tablespoon butter
- 1 pound pork chops, bone in
- 1 tablespoon grainy mustard
- 1 tablespoon yellow mustard
- 2 tablespoons mayonnaise
- 1 tablespoon BBQ sauce
- ½ tablespoon honey
- ½ tablespoon lime juice

Directions:
In your slow cooker, mix butter with pork chops, grainy mustard, yellow mustard, mayonnaise, BBQ sauce, honey and limejuice, stir, cover and cook on High for 4 hours. Divide pork chops and mustard sauce between plates and serve with a side salad.
Enjoy!

Nutrition: calories 300, fat 8, fiber 10, carbs 16, protein 16

Easy Leeks and Fennel Soup

Preparation time: 10 minutes
Cooking time: 4 hours
Servings: 2

Ingredients:
- 1 fennel bulb, chopped
- 1 leek, chopped
- 1 and ½ cups veggie stock
- ½ teaspoon cumin, ground
- ½ tablespoon olive oil
- Salt and black pepper to the taste

Directions:
In your slow cooker, mix fennel with leek, stock, cumin, oil, salt and pepper, stir, cover, cook on High for 4 hours, ladle into bowls and serve hot.
Enjoy!

Nutrition: calories 132, fat 2, fiber 5, carbs 11, protein 3

Beef and Artichoke Soup

Preparation time: 10 minutes
Cooking time: 8 hours
Servings: 2

Ingredients:
- 1 celery stalk, chopped
- ½ pound beef stew meat, cubed
- 1 small carrot, chopped
- 1 small yellow onion, chopped
- 1 garlic clove, minced
- ¼ teaspoon oregano, dried
- ¼ teaspoon rosemary, dried
- ¼ teaspoon fennel seeds
- ¼ teaspoon thyme, dried
- A pinch of red pepper flakes
- A pinch of garlic powder
- A pinch of salt and black pepper
- 20 ounces canned artichoke hearts, drained and chopped
- 2 and ½ cups veggie stock

Directions:
In your slow cooker, mix beef with celery, carrot, onion, garlic, oregano, rosemary, fennel seeds, thyme, pepper flakes, garlic powder, salt, pepper, stock and artichokes, stir, cover, cook on Low for 8 hours, ladle into bowls and serve.
Enjoy!

Nutrition: calories 362, fat 3, fiber 5, carbs 16, protein 5

Veggie Stew

Preparation time: 10 minutes
Cooking time: 8 hours
Servings: 4

Ingredients:
- 1 tablespoon olive oil
- ½ green bell pepper, chopped
- ½ yellow onion, chopped
- ½ celery stalks, chopped
- 1 garlic cloves, minced
- 6 ounces canned tomatoes, chopped
- 1 cup veggie stock
- Salt and black pepper to the taste
- 4 ounces white mushrooms, sliced
- 4 ounces canned kidney beans, drained
- 1 small zucchini, chopped
- ½ tablespoon Cajun seasoning

Directions:
In your slow cooker, mix oil with bell pepper, onion, celery, garlic, tomatoes, stock, mushrooms, beans, zucchini, Cajun seasoning, salt and pepper, stir, cover and cook on Low for 8 hours Divide into bowls and serve your stew hot.
Enjoy!

Nutrition: calories 272, fat 4, fiber 7, carbs 19, protein 7

Eggplant Stew

Preparation time: 10 minutes
Cooking time: 8 hours
Servings: 2

Ingredients:
- 12 ounces canned tomatoes, chopped
- 1 small red onion, chopped
- 1 red bell pepper, chopped
- 1 small eggplant, roughly chopped
- ½ tablespoon smoked paprika
- 1 teaspoon cumin, ground
- Salt and black pepper to the taste
- Juice of ½ lemon
- ½ tablespoon parsley, chopped

Directions:
In your slow cooker, mix tomatoes with onion, bell peppers, eggplant, smoked paprika, cumin, salt, pepper and lemon juice, stir, cover, cook on Low for 8 hours, divide into bowls and serve with parsley sprinkled on top.
Enjoy!

Nutrition: calories 261, fat 4, fiber 6, carbs 14, protein 7

Lentils Stew

Preparation time: 10 minutes
Cooking time: 5 hours
Servings: 2

Ingredients:
- 1 and ½ cups water
- ½ cup red lentils
- 6 ounces canned tomatoes, chopped
- 1 small yellow onion, chopped
- 1 garlic clove, minced
- 1 teaspoon turmeric powder
- ¼ tablespoons ginger, grated
- 1 cardamom pods
- 1 bay leaf
- ½ teaspoons mustard seeds
- ½ teaspoons onion seeds
- ¼ teaspoons fenugreek seeds
- ¼ teaspoon fennel seeds
- Salt and black pepper to the taste

Directions:
In your slow cooker, mix water with lentils, tomatoes, onion, garlic, turmeric, ginger, cardamom, bay leaf, mustard seeds, onion seeds, fenugreek seeds, fennel seeds, salt and pepper, stir, cover, cook on High for 5 hours, divide into bowls and serve.
Enjoy!

Nutrition: calories 303, fat 4, fiber 8, carbs 12, protein 4

Slow Cooker Side Dish Recipes For 2

Creamy Scalloped Tater Tots

Preparation time: 10 minutes
Cooking time: 3 hours
Servings: 2

Ingredients:
- ½ pound tater tots, cubed
- 2 ounces cream of chicken soup
- 2 tablespoons milk
- ¼ cup cheddar cheese, shredded
- 1 tablespoon butter, melted
- Cooking spray
- 1 yellow onion, chopped
- Salt and black pepper to the taste

Directions:
Grease your slow cooker with cooking spray, add tater tots with cream of chicken, milk, cheese, butter, onion, salt and pepper, toss well, cover and cook on High for 3 hours. Divide between plates and serve as a side dish.
Enjoy!

Nutrition: calories 300, fat 14, fiber 6, carbs 22, protein 6

Quick Broccoli Side Dish

Preparation time: 10 minutes
Cooking time: 3 hours
Servings: 2

Ingredients:
- 2 cups broccoli florets
- 2 ounces cream of celery soup
- 2 tablespoons cheddar cheese, shredded
- 1 small yellow onion, chopped
- ¼ teaspoon Worcestershire sauce
- Salt and black pepper to the taste
- 10 butter flavored crackers, crushed
- ½ tablespoon butter

Directions:
In your slow cooker, mix broccoli with cream of celery, cheddar cheese, onion, Worcestershire sauce, salt, pepper and butter and toss. Sprinkle crackers on top, cover, cook on High for 3 hours, divide between plates and serve as a side dish.
Enjoy!

Nutrition: calories 162, fat 11, fiber 2, carbs 11, protein 5

Delicious Bean Mix

Preparation time: 10 minutes
Cooking time: 5 hours
Servings: 2

Ingredients:
- ½ cup ketchup
- ½ celery rib, chopped
- 1 small yellow onion, chopped
- ½ red bell pepper, chopped
- ½ sweet red pepper, chopped
- 1 tablespoon brown sugar
- 2 tablespoons water
- 2 tablespoons Italian salad dressing
- ¼ tablespoon cider vinegar
- ¼ teaspoon mustard
- Salt and black pepper to the taste
- 3 ounces canned kidney beans, drained
- 3 ounces canned black-eyed peas, drained
- 3 ounces canned great northern beans, drained
- 2 ounces canned corn, drained
- 2 ounces lima beans, drained
- 2 ounces black beans, drained

Directions:
In your slow cooker, mix ketchup with celery, onion, red bell pepper, sweet red pepper, brown sugar, water, Italian salad dressing, vinegar, mustard, salt, pepper, kidney beans, black-eyed peas, great northern beans, corn, lima beans and black beans, toss a bit, cover and cook on Low for 5 hours. Divide between plates and serve as a side dish.
Enjoy!

Nutrition: calories 255, fat 6, fiber 7, carbs 38, protein 7

Easy Green Beans Mix

Preparation time: 10 minutes
Cooking time: 2 hours
Servings: 2

Ingredients:
- 4 cups green beans, trimmed
- 2 tablespoons butter, melted
- 2 tablespoons brown sugar
- Salt and black pepper to the taste
- ¼ teaspoon soy sauce

Directions:
In your slow cooker, mix green beans with butter, brown sugar, salt, pepper and soy sauce, toss, cover and cook on Low for 2 hours. Divide between plates and serve as a side dish.
Enjoy!

Nutrition: calories 236, fat 6, fiber 8, carbs 10, protein 6

Creamy Corn Side Dish

Preparation time: 10 minutes
Cooking time: 4 hours
Servings: 2

Ingredients:
- 3 cups corn
- 2 ounces cream cheese, cubed
- 2 tablespoons milk
- 2 tablespoon whipping cream
- 2 tablespoons butter, melted
- Salt and black pepper to the taste
- 2 bacon strips, cooked and crumbled
- 1 tablespoon green onions, chopped

Directions:
In your slow cooker, mix corn with cream cheese, milk, whipping cream, butter, salt and pepper, toss, cover and cook on Low for 4 hours. Divide between plates, sprinkle bacon and green onions on top and serve as a side dish.
Enjoy!

Nutrition: calories 261, fat 11, fiber 3, carbs 17, protein 6

Tasty Peas and Carrots

Preparation time: 10 minutes
Cooking time: 5 hours
Servings: 2

Ingredients:
- ¼ pound carrots, sliced
- 1 small yellow onion, chopped
- 2 tablespoons water
- 2 tablespoons butter
- 1 tablespoon honey
- 2 garlic cloves, minced
- ¼ teaspoon marjoram, dried
- Salt and black pepper to the taste
- 3 ounces peas

Directions:
In your slow cooker, mix carrots with onion, water, butter, honey, garlic, marjoram, salt, pepper and peas, stir, cover and cook on Low for 5 hours. Divide between plates and serve as a side dish.
Enjoy!

Nutrition: calories 100, fat 4, fiber 3, carbs 15, protein 4

Corn Chowder

Preparation time: 10 minutes
Cooking time: 8 hours
Servings: 2

Ingredients:
- 1 small yellow onion, chopped
- 1 tablespoon olive oil
- ½ red bell pepper, chopped
- 1 cup gold potatoes, chopped
- 1 cup corn kernels
- 2 cups veggie stock
- ¼ teaspoon sweet paprika
- ½ teaspoon cumin, ground
- 1 scallion, chopped
- Salt and black pepper to the taste
- ½ cup milk

Directions:
Heat up a pan with the oil over medium-high heat, add onion, stir, cook for a few minutes and transfer to your slow cooker. Add bell pepper, potatoes, corn, stock, paprika, cumin, salt and pepper, stir, cover and cook on Low for 7 hours and 30 minutes. Blend soup using an immersion blender, add milk, blend again, cover pot and cook on Low for 30 minutes more. Ladle soup into bowls, sprinkle scallions on top and serve.
Enjoy!

Nutrition: calories 312, fat 4, fiber 6, carbs 12, protein 6

Mushroom Rice

Preparation time: 10 minutes
Cooking time: 3 hours
Servings: 2

Ingredients:
- ½ cup rice
- 2 green onions, chopped
- 1 garlic clove, minced
- ¼ pound baby Portobello mushrooms, sliced
- 1 cup beef stock

Directions:
In your slow cooker, mix rice with onions, garlic, mushrooms and stock, stir, cover and cook on Low for 3 hours. Stir rice, divide between plates and serve as a side dish.
Enjoy!

Nutrition: calories 200, fat 6, fiber 4, carbs 28, protein 5

Butternut Mix

Preparation time: 10 minutes
Cooking time: 4 hours
Servings: 2

Ingredients:
- ¼ cup carrots, sliced
- 1 small yellow onion, chopped
- ½ tablespoon olive oil
- ½ teaspoon brown sugar
- ½ teaspoon curry powder
- 1 garlic clove, minced
- A pinch of cinnamon powder
- A pinch of ginger, ground
- A pinch of salt and black pepper
- 1 small butternut squash, cubed
- 1 cup veggie stock
- ½ cup coconut milk
- ¼ cup basmati rice

Directions:
In your slow cooker, mix carrots with onion, oil, sugar, curry powder, garlic, cinnamon, ginger, salt, pepper, squash, stock, milk and rice, stir, cover and cook on Low for 4 hours. Divide between plates and serve as a side dish.
Enjoy!

Nutrition: calories 200, fat 5, fiber 7, carbs 28, protein 4

Easy Potatoes Mix

Preparation time: 10 minutes
Cooking time: 6 hours
Servings: 2

Ingredients:
- 4 small red potatoes, peeled and halved
- 1 celery rib, chopped
- ½ carrot, chopped
- 1 small yellow onion, chopped
- ½ cup chicken stock
- ½ tablespoon parsley, chopped
- Salt and black pepper to the taste
- ½ tablespoon butter
- 1 garlic clove, minced

Directions:
In your slow cooker, mix potatoes with celery, carrot, onion, stock, butter, garlic, salt and pepper, stir a bit, cover and cook on Low for 6 hours. Divide between plates, sprinkle parsley on top and serve as a side dish.
Enjoy!

Nutrition: calories 114, fat 4, fiber 4, carbs 18, protein 4

Beans and Spinach Mix

Preparation time: 10 minutes
Cooking time: 4 hours
Servings: 2

Ingredients:
- 2 carrots, sliced
- ½ cup northern beans, dried
- 1 garlic clove, minced
- 1 small yellow onion, chopped
- Salt and black pepper to the taste
- ¼ teaspoon oregano, dried
- 2 ounces baby spinach
- 1 cup veggie stock
- 1 teaspoon lemon peel, grated
- 1 tablespoons lemon juice
- 1 small avocado, pitted, peeled and chopped
- 2 tablespoons pistachios, chopped

Directions:
In your slow cooker, mix beans with onion, carrots, garlic, salt, pepper, oregano and veggie stock, stir, cover and cook on High for 4 hours. Add spinach, lemon juice and lemon peel, stir and leave aside for 5 minutes. Transfer beans, carrots and spinach mix to a bowl, add pistachios and avocado, toss, divide between plates and serve as a side dish.
Enjoy!

Nutrition: calories 219, fat 8, fiber 14, carbs 15, protein 17

Creamy Potatoes

Preparation time: 10 minutes
Cooking time: 4 hours
Servings: 2

Ingredients:
- Cooking spray
- ½ pound gold potatoes, halved and sliced
- 1 small yellow onion, cut into medium wedges
- 2 ounces canned potato cream soup
- 2 ounces coconut milk
- 1 cup cream cheese, cubed
- ¼ cup veggie stock
- Salt and black pepper to the taste
- 1 tablespoons parsley, chopped

Directions:
Grease your slow cooker with cooking spray, add half of the potatoes on the bottom, add onion pieces, half of the cream soup, cream cheese, coconut milk, salt and pepper. Add the rest of the potatoes, cream, coconut milk, cream cheese and stock, cover and cook on High for 4 hours. Sprinkle parsley on top, divide potatoes between plates and serve as a side dish.
Enjoy!

Nutrition: calories 306, fat 14, fiber 4, carbs 15, protein 12

Sweet Potatoes and Orange Mix

Preparation time: 10 minutes
Cooking time: 3 hours
Servings: 2

Ingredients:
- ½ pound sweet potatoes, thinly sliced
- ½ tablespoon sugar
- 2 tablespoons orange juice
- A pinch of salt and black pepper
- ¼ teaspoon thyme, dried
- ¼ teaspoon sage, dried
- ½ tablespoon olive oil

Directions:
Arrange potato slices in your slow cooker. In a bowl, mix orange juice with salt, pepper, sugar, thyme, sage and oil, whisk well, add over potatoes, cover slow cooker and cook on High for 3 hours. Divide between plates and serve as a side dish.
Enjoy!

Nutrition: calories 189, fat 4, fiber 4, carbs 17, protein 4

Cauliflower and Broccoli Mix

Preparation time: 10 minutes
Cooking time: 3 hours
Servings: 2

Ingredients:
- 1 cup broccoli florets
- 1 cup cauliflower florets
- 2 ounces tomato paste
- 1 small yellow onion, chopped
- ¼ teaspoon thyme, dried
- Salt and black pepper to the taste
- 1 tablespoon almonds, sliced

Directions:
1. In your slow cooker, mix broccoli with cauliflower, tomato paste, onion, thyme, salt and pepper, toss, cover and cook on High for 3 hours.
2. Add almonds, toss, divide between plates and serve as a side dish.

Enjoy!

Nutrition: calories 177, fat 12, fiber 7, carbs 20, protein 7

Mushroom Risotto

Preparation time: 10 minutes
Cooking time: 1 hour and 30 minutes
Servings: 2

Ingredients:
- 1 small shallot, chopped
- 2 ounces white mushrooms, sliced
- 1 tablespoons olive oil
- ½ teaspoon garlic, minced
- Salt and black pepper to the taste
- ½ cup white rice
- 1 and ½ cups veggie stock
- 2 tablespoons peas

Directions:
In your slow cooker, mix oil with shallot, mushrooms, garlic, rice, stock, peas, salt and pepper, stir, cover, cook on High for 1 hour and 30 minutes, divide between plates and serve as a side dish.
Enjoy!

Nutrition: calories 204, fat 7, fiber 3, carbs 17, protein 7

Curried Veggie Side Dish

Preparation time: 10 minutes
Cooking time: 3 hours
Servings: 2

Ingredients:
- 2 ounces yellow summer squash, peeled and roughly chopped
- 2 ounces zucchini, halved and sliced
- ½ cups button mushrooms, quartered
- 1 small red sweet potatoes, chopped
- ½ leek, sliced
- ½ tablespoons veggie stock
- 1 garlic cloves, minced
- ¼ tablespoon Thai red curry paste
- ¼ tablespoon ginger, grated
- Salt and black pepper to the taste
- 2 tablespoons coconut milk
- 1 tablespoon basil, chopped

Directions:
In your slow cooker, mix zucchini with summer squash, mushrooms, red pepper, leeks, garlic, stock, curry paste, ginger, coconut milk, salt, pepper and basil, toss, cover, cook on Low for 3 hours, divide between plates and serve as a side dish.
Enjoy!

Nutrition: calories 169, fat 2, fiber 2, carbs 15, protein 6

Rosemary Potatoes

Preparation time: 10 minutes
Cooking time: 3 hours
Servings: 2

Ingredients:
- ½ tablespoons olive oil
- ½ pound new potatoes, halved
- 2 garlic cloves, minced
- Salt and black pepper to the taste
- ¼ tablespoon rosemary, chopped

Directions:
In your slow cooker, mix oil with potatoes, garlic, rosemary, salt and pepper, toss, cover, cook on High for 3 hours, divide between plates and serve as a side dish.
Enjoy!

Nutrition: calories 202, fat 2, fiber 6, carbs 18, protein 8

Maple and Thyme Brussels Sprouts

Preparation time: 10 minutes
Cooking time: 3 hours
Servings: 2

Ingredients:
- 1 small red onion, chopped
- ½ pounds Brussels sprouts, trimmed and halved
- A pinch of salt and black pepper
- 2 tablespoons apple juice
- 1 tablespoons olive oil
- 2 tablespoons maple syrup
- 1 tablespoon thyme, chopped

Directions:
In your slow cooker, mix sprouts with onion, salt, pepper and apple juice, toss, cover and cook on Low for 3 hours. In a bowl, mix maple syrup with oil and thyme, whisk really well, add over Brussels sprouts, toss, divide between plates and serve as a side dish.
Enjoy!

Nutrition: calories 170, fat 4, fiber 4, carbs 14, protein 6

Potatoes and Apples Mix

Preparation time: 10 minutes
Cooking time: 7 hours
Servings: 2

Ingredients:
- 1 small green apple, cored and cut into wedges
- ½ pound sweet potatoes, cut into medium wedges
- 1 tablespoon whipping cream
- 2 tablespoons cherries, dried
- 2 tablespoons apple butter
- ½ teaspoon pumpkin pie spice

Directions:
In your slow cooker, mix potatoes with green apples, cream, cherries, apple butter and spice, toss, cover, cook on Low for 7 hours, divide between plates and serve as a side dish.
Enjoy!

Nutrition: calories 351, fat 8, fiber 5, carbs 48, protein 7

Chili Black Beans Mix

Preparation time: 10 minutes
Cooking time: 10 hours
Servings: 2

Ingredients:
- ½ pound black beans, soaked overnight and drained
- A pinch of salt and black pepper
- 1 and ½ cups veggie stock
- 1 cup yellow onion, chopped
- ½ tablespoon canned chipotle chili pepper in adobo sauce
- 2 garlic cloves, minced
- ½ tablespoon lime juice
- 2 tablespoons cilantro, chopped
- 2 tablespoons pumpkin seeds

Directions:
Put the beans in your slow cooker, add salt, black pepper, onion, stock, garlic and chipotle chili, stir, cover and cook on Low for 10 hours. Add lime juice and cilantro, mash beans a bit using a potato masher, divide between plates and serve with pumpkin seeds on top.
Enjoy!

Nutrition: calories 200, fat 3, fiber 4, carbs 7, protein 5

Simple Carrots Mix

Preparation time: 10 minutes
Cooking time: 8 hours
Servings: 2

Ingredients:
- ½ pound carrots, sliced
- A pinch of salt and black pepper
- ½ tablespoons water
- 2 tablespoons sugar
- ½ tablespoon olive oil
- ½ teaspoon orange rind, grated

Directions:
Put the oil in your slow cooker, add the carrots, water, sugar, salt, pepper and orange rind, toss, cover and cook on Low for 8 hours. Divide between plates and serve as a side dish.
Enjoy!

Nutrition: calories 140, fat 2, fiber 2, carbs 7, protein 6

Hot Beans and Lentils

Preparation time: 10 minutes
Cooking time: 8 hours
Servings: 2

Ingredients:
- 1 tablespoon thyme, chopped
- ½ tablespoon olive oil
- 1 small yellow onion, chopped
- 2 cups water
- 2 garlic cloves, minced
- 1 tablespoon cider vinegar
- 2 tablespoons tomato paste
- 2 tablespoons maple syrup
- 1 tablespoon soy sauce
- 1 tablespoons red chili paste
- 1 tablespoon dry mustard
- 1 cup great northern beans, dried
- ¼ cup red lentils, dried

Directions:
In your slow cooker, mix oil with thyme, onion, water, garlic, vinegar, tomato paste, maple syrup, sauce, chili paste, mustard, beans and lentils, stir well, cover and cook on Low for 8 hours. Divide between plates and serve as a side dish.
Enjoy!

Nutrition: calories 200, fat 2, fiber 4, carbs 7, protein 8

Wild Rice Mix

Preparation time: 10 minutes
Cooking time: 6 hours
Servings: 2

Ingredients:
- 10 ounces veggie stock
- 1 carrot, shredded
- 1 cup wild rice
- 1 ounce mushrooms, sliced
- 1 tablespoon olive oil
- ½ teaspoons marjoram, dried
- A pinch of salt and black pepper
- 1 tablespoon cherries, dried
- 1 tablespoon pecans, chopped
- 1 tablespoon green onions, chopped

Directions:
Put the stock in your slow cooker, add rice, carrots, mushrooms, oil, salt, pepper and marjoram, stir, cover and cook on Low for 6 hours. Add cherries and green onions, stir, cover slow cooker, leave rice mix aside for a few minutes, divide between plates and serve with chopped pecans on top.
Enjoy!

Nutrition: calories 200, fat 2, fiber 3, carbs 7, protein 5

Mashed Potatoes

Preparation time: 10 minutes
Cooking time: 6 hours
Servings: 2

Ingredients:
- 1 pound russet potatoes, peeled and cubed
- 2 garlic cloves, chopped
- 3 ounces veggie stock
- 1 bay leaf
- ¼ cup milk
- 2 tablespoons butter
- A pinch of salt and white pepper

Directions:
Put potatoes in your slow cooker, add stock, garlic and bay leaf, stir, cover and cook on Low for 6 hours. Drain potatoes, discard bay leaf, return them to your slow cooker, mash using a potato masher, add milk, butter, salt and pepper, whisk really well, divide between plates and serve as a side dish.
Enjoy!

Nutrition: calories 135, fat 4, fiber 2, carbs 10, protein 4

Squash Mix

Preparation time: 10 minutes
Cooking time: 7 hours
Servings: 2

Ingredients:
- 1 butternut squash, peeled and cubed
- 1 small yellow onion, cut into medium wedges
- 3 ounces spinach
- 2 tablespoons barley
-
- 3 ounces veggie stock
- ¼ cup water
- A pinch of salt and black pepper
- 1 garlic clove, minced

Directions:
Put squash in your slow cooker, add barley, spinach, stock, water, onion, garlic, salt and pepper, stir, cover and cook on Low for 7 hours. Divide between plates and serve as a side dish.
Enjoy!

Nutrition: calories 160, fat 3, fiber 7, carbs 13, protein 7

Beans and Sauce

Preparation time: 10 minutes
Cooking time: 8 hours
Servings: 2

Ingredients:
- ½ pound lima beans, soaked for 6 hours and drained
- 1 celery ribs, chopped
- 1 tablespoon olive oil
- 1 yellow onions, chopped
- 1 carrot, chopped
- 2 tablespoons tomato paste
- 1 garlic cloves, minced
- A pinch of salt and black pepper to the taste
- 3 cups water
- 1 bay leaf
- ½ teaspoon oregano, dried
- ¼ teaspoon thyme, dried
- A pinch of red pepper, crushed
- 2 tablespoons parsley, chopped

Directions:
In your slow cooker, mix oil with onions, garlic, celery, carrots, salt, pepper, beans, tomato paste, water, bay leaf, oregano, thyme and red pepper, stir, cover and cook on Low for 8 hours. Add parsley, stir, divide between plates and serve as a side dish/
Enjoy!

Nutrition: calories 160, fat 3, fiber 7, carbs 9, protein 12

Hot Beans

Preparation time: 10 minutes
Cooking time: 2 hours
Servings: 2

Ingredients:
- 2 ounces canned white beans, drained
- 2 tablespoons hot sauce
- 2 tablespoons cream cheese, cubed
- 2 tablespoons coconut milk
- ¼ teaspoon cumin, ground
- ¼ tablespoon chili powder

Directions:
Put beans in your slow cooker, add hot sauce, cream cheese, coconut milk, cumin and chili powder, stir, cover and cook for 2 hours. Divide between plates and serve right away as a side dish.
Enjoy!

Nutrition: calories 230, fat 4, fiber 6, carbs 8, protein 10

Flavored Potato and Spinach Mix

Preparation time: 10 minutes
Cooking time: 3 hours
Servings: 2

Ingredients:
- 4 gold potatoes, peeled and roughly chopped
- ½ tablespoon olive oil
- 1 tablespoons water
- 1 small yellow onion, chopped
- ¼ teaspoon coriander, ground
- ¼ teaspoon cumin, ground
- ¼ teaspoon garam masala
- ¼ teaspoon chili powder
- Salt and black pepper to the taste
- ¼ pound spinach, roughly torn

Directions:
Put the potatoes in your slow cooker, add oil, water, onion, stock, coriander, cumin, garam masala, chili powder, black pepper and spinach, stir, cover and cook on High for 3 hours. Divide between plates and serve as a side dish.
Enjoy!

Nutrition: calories 270, fat 4, fiber 6, carbs 8, protein 12

Baked Beans

Preparation time: 10 minutes
Cooking time: 12 hours
Servings: 2

Ingredients:
- ¼ pound navy beans, soaked overnight and drained
- 1 tablespoon maple syrup
- 1 tablespoon bourbon
- 1 tablespoon bbq sauce
- 1 tablespoon sugar
- 1 tablespoon ketchup
- 1 tablespoon water
- 1 tablespoon mustard
- 1 tablespoon blackstrap molasses
- 1 tablespoon apple cider vinegar
- 1 tablespoon olive oil
- 1 tablespoon soy sauce

Directions:
Put the beans in your slow cooker, add maple syrup, bourbon, bbq sauce, sugar, ketchup, water, mustard, molasses, vinegar, oil and soy sauce , stir everything, cover and cook on Low for 12 hours. Divide between plates and serve as a side dish.
Enjoy!

Nutrition: calories 430, fat 7, fiber 8, carbs 15, protein 19

White Bean Mix

Preparation time: 10 minutes
Cooking time: 6 hours
Servings: 4

Ingredients:
- 1 celery stalk, chopped
- 1 leek, sliced
- 2 garlic cloves, minced
- 1 carrot, chopped
- 1 cup veggie stock
- 6 ounces canned tomatoes, chopped
- 1 bay leaf
- ½ tablespoon Italian seasoning
- 15 ounces canned white beans, drained

For the breadcrumbs:
- Zest of ½ lemon, grated
- 1 garlic clove, minced
- 1 tablespoon olive oil
- ½ cup breadcrumbs
- 1 tablespoon parsley, chopped

Directions:
In your slow cooker, mix celery with leek, 2 garlic cloves, carrot, stock, tomatoes, bay leaf, Italian seasoning and beans, stir, cover and cook on Low for 6 hours. Heat up a pan with the oil over medium-high heat, add breadcrumbs, lemon zest, 1 garlic clove and parsley, stir and toast for a couple of minutes. Divide white beans on plates, sprinkle breadcrumbs mix on top and serve as a side dish.
Enjoy!

Nutrition: calories 223, fat 3, fiber 7, carbs 10, protein 7

Mixed Veggies Side Dish

Preparation time: 10 minutes
Cooking time: 4 hours and 30 minutes
Servings: 2

Ingredients:
- 1 sweet potato, cubed
- 1 small yellow onion, chopped
- 1 small cauliflower head, florets separated
- 5 ounces canned coconut milk
- 1 teaspoons sriracha sauce
- 1 and ½ tablespoons soy sauce
- A pinch of salt and black pepper
- ½ tablespoon sugar
- 1 and ½ tablespoons red curry paste
- ½ cup green peas
- 3 ounces white mushrooms, roughly chopped
- 2 tablespoons cashews, toasted and chopped
- 2 tablespoons cilantro, chopped

Directions:
Put coconut milk in your slow cooker, add potatoes, onion, cauliflower florets, sriracha sauce, soy sauce, salt, pepper, curry paste and sugar, stir, cover and cook on Low for 4 hours. Add mushrooms, peas and cilantro, stir, cover and cook on Low for 30 minutes more. Divide between plates and serve as a side dish.
Enjoy!

Nutrition: calories 200, fat 3, fiber 5, carbs 15, protein 12

Cabbage and Apples Mix

Preparation time: 10 minutes
Cooking time: 6 hours
Servings: 2

Ingredients:
- 1 small onion, sliced
- 1 small cabbage, shredded
- 1 apples, peeled, cored and roughly chopped
- A pinch of salt and black pepper to the taste
- ½ cup apple juice
- ¼ cup chicken stock
- 1 and ½ tablespoons mustard
- ½ tablespoon olive oil

Directions:
Grease your slow cooker with the oil, add apples, cabbage and onions. In a bowl, mix stock with mustard, salt, black pepper and the apple juice, whisk well, pour into the cooker, cover and cook on Low for 6 hours. Divide between plates and serve as a side dish.
Enjoy!

Nutrition: calories 200, fat 4, fiber 2, carbs 8, protein 6

Flavored Mushroom Mix

Preparation time: 10 minutes
Cooking time: 4 hours
Servings: 2

Ingredients:
- 1 bay leaf
- 2 garlic cloves, minced
- 12 ounces mushroom caps
- A pinch of thyme dried
- A pinch of basil, dried
- A pinch of oregano, dried
- ½ cup veggie stock
- Salt and black pepper to the taste
- 1 tablespoon olive oil
- 1 tablespoon parsley, chopped

Directions:
Grease your slow cooker with the olive oil, add mushrooms, garlic, bay leaves, thyme, basil, oregano, black pepper and stock. Cover and cook on Low for 4 hours. Divide between plates and serve with parsley sprinkled on top as a side dish.
Enjoy!

Nutrition: calories 122, fat 6, fiber 1, carbs 8, protein 5

Squash and Sauce

Preparation time: 10 minutes
Cooking time: 7 hours
Servings: 2

Ingredients:
- 2 tablespoons raisins
- 1 acorn squash, peeled and cut into medium wedges
- 7 ounces canned cranberry sauce, unsweetened
- A pinch of cinnamon powder
- A pinch of salt and black pepper

Directions:
Put acorn in your slow cooker, add cranberry sauce, raisins, cinnamon, salt and pepper, stir, cover and cook on Low for 7 hours. Divide between plates and serve as a side dish.
Enjoy!

Nutrition: calories 230, fat 3, fiber 3, carbs 10, protein 2

Zucchini and Squash Mix

Preparation time: 10 minutes
Cooking time: 6 hours
Servings: 2

Ingredients:
- 1 cup zucchinis, sliced
- ½ teaspoon Italian seasoning
- Salt and black pepper
- 1 cup yellow squash, peeled and cut into wedges
- ½ teaspoon garlic powder
- 1 tablespoon olive oil

Directions:
Put the oil in your slow cooker, add zucchini and squash, Italian seasoning, black pepper, salt and garlic powder, toss well, cover and cook on Low for 6 hours. Divide between plates and serve as a side dish.
Enjoy!

Nutrition: calories 170, fat 2, fiber 4, carbs 8, protein 5

Simple Kale Side Dish

Preparation time: 10 minutes
Cooking time: 6 hours
Servings: 2

Ingredients:
- 2 ounces ham hock slices
- ½ cup water
- ½ cup chicken stock
- 6 cups kale leaves, torn
- A pinch of salt and cayenne pepper
- 1 tablespoon olive oil
- 1 small yellow onion, chopped
- 1 tablespoon apple cider vinegar

Directions:
Put ham in a heatproof bowl, add the water and the stock, cover and microwave for 3 minutes. Heat up a pan with the oil over medium-high heat, add onion, stir and cook for 5 minutes. Drain ham, transfer it to your slow cooker, and add sautéed onions, kale, salt, cayenne and vinegar, toss, cover and cook on Low for 6 hours. Divide between plates and serve as a side dish.
Enjoy!

Nutrition: calories 200, fat 4, fiber 7, carbs 10, protein 3

Cheesy Spinach

Preparation time: 10 minutes
Cooking time: 5 hours
Servings: 2

Ingredients:
- 10 ounces spinach
- 1 cup heavy cream
- ½ cup cream cheese, cubed
- 2 tablespoons butter, melted

Directions:
In your slow cooker, mix spinach with cream, butter and cream cheese, stir, cover and cook on Low for 5 hours. Divide between plates and serve as a side dish.
Enjoy!

Nutrition: calories 230, fat 12, fiber 2, carbs 9, protein 12

Simple Sweet Potatoes Mix

Preparation time: 10 minutes
Cooking time: 6 hours
Servings: 2

Ingredients:
- 2 sweet potatoes, peeled and cut into medium slices
- 1 tablespoon orange juice
- ½ tablespoon sugar
- A pinch of salt and black pepper
- ¼ teaspoon sage, dried
- A pinch of thyme, dried
- ½ tablespoon butter, melted
- 2 bacon slices, cooked and crumbled

Directions:
Place sweet potatoes in your slow cooker. In a bowl, mix orange juice with sugar, salt, pepper, sage, thyme and butter, whisk really well, add this over sweet potatoes, also add bacon, cover and cook on Low for 6 hours. Divide between plates and serve as a side dish.
Enjoy!

Nutrition: calories 209, fat 4, fiber 4, carbs 29, protein 4

Cauliflower Mash

Preparation time: 10 minutes
Cooking time: 5 hours
Servings: 2

Ingredients:
- 1 small cauliflower head, florets separated
- 1 tablespoon dill, chopped
- 2 garlic cloves
- 1 tablespoons butter, melted
- A pinch of salt and black pepper

Directions:
Put cauliflower in your slow cooker, add garlic and water to cover cauliflower, cover and cook on High for 5 hours. Drain cauliflower, add dill, salt, pepper and butter, mash using a potato masher, whisk well and serve as a side dish.
Enjoy!

Nutrition: calories 187, fat 4, fiber 5, carbs 7, protein 3

Veggie Mix

Preparation time: 10 minutes
Cooking time: 5 hours
Servings: 2

Ingredients:
- 1 eggplant, cubed
- 1 celery stalks, chopped
- ¼ pound plum tomatoes, chopped
- 1 small zucchini, halved and sliced
- ½ red bell pepper, chopped
- 1 small sweet onion, chopped
- 1 tablespoon tomato paste
- 1 tablespoon raisins
- ½ tablespoon sugar
- A pinch of red pepper flakes, crushed
- 1 tablespoon basil, chopped
- 1 tablespoon parsley, chopped
- A pinch of salt and black pepper
- 1 tablespoon green olives, pitted and chopped
- 1 tablespoon capers
- 1 tablespoon red wine vinegar

Directions:
In your slow cooker, mix eggplants with celery, tomatoes, zucchini, bell pepper, sweet onion, tomato paste, raisins, stevia, pepper flakes, basil, parsley, salt, pepper, olives, capers and vinegar, stir, cover and cook on Low for 5 hours. Divide between plates and serve as a side dish.
Enjoy!

Nutrition: calories 100, fat 1, fiber 2, carbs 7, protein 5

Rice and Farro Pilaf

Preparation time: 10 minutes
Cooking time: 4 hours
Servings: 2

Ingredients:
- 1 small shallot, chopped
- ½ teaspoon garlic, minced
- A drizzle of olive oil
- ½ cup whole grain farro
- ½ cup wild rice
- 2 cups chicken stock
- Salt and black pepper to the taste
- ½ tablespoon parsley, chopped
- 1 tablespoon hazelnuts, toasted and chopped
- 1 tablespoon cherries, dried

Directions:
Grease your slow cooker with the oil, add shallot, garlic, farro, rice, stock, salt, pepper, cherries and hazelnuts, stir, cover and cook on Low for 4 hours. Add parsley, stir, divide between plates and serve as a side dish.
Enjoy!

Nutrition: calories 152, fat 4, fiber 5, carbs 20, protein 4

Quinoa Pilaf

Preparation time: 10 minutes
Cooking time: 1 hour and 30 minutes
Servings: 2

Ingredients:
- 1 cup quinoa
- 1 garlic clove, minced
- 1 tablespoon olive oil
- Salt to the taste
- 1 teaspoon turmeric powder
- 1 and ½ cups water
- 1 tablespoon parsley, chopped
- 1 teaspoon cumin, ground

Directions:
Grease your slow cooker with the oil, add quinoa, garlic, salt, turmeric, water and cumin, stir, cover and cook on High for 1 hour and 30 minutes. Add parsley, stir, divide between plates and serve as a side dish.
Enjoy!

Nutrition: calories 152, fat 3, fiber 6, carbs 8, protein 4

Moroccan Risotto

Preparation time: 10 minutes
Cooking time: 2 hours
Servings: 2

Ingredients:
- ½ tablespoon olive oil
- ¼ teaspoon saffron threads, crushed
- 1 small yellow onion, chopped
- 1 tablespoon milk, hot
- 1 cup Arborio rice
- 2 cups veggie stock
- A pinch of salt and black pepper
- ½ tablespoon honey
- A pinch of cinnamon powder
- 1 tablespoon almonds, chopped

Directions:
In a bowl, mix milk with saffron, stir and leave aside for a few minutes. In your slow cooker, mix oil with onions, rice, stock, saffron, milk, honey, salt, pepper, cinnamon and almonds, stir, cover and cook on High for 2 hours. Divide between plates and serve as a side dish.
Enjoy!

Nutrition: calories 251, fat 4, fiber 7, carbs 29, protein 4

Farro Pilaf

Preparation time: 10 minutes
Cooking time: 4 hours
Servings: 2

Ingredients:
- ½ tablespoon apple cider vinegar
- ½ cup whole grain farro
- ½ teaspoon lemon juice
- Salt to the taste
- 1 and ½ cups water
- ½ tablespoon olive oil
- 1 tablespoon cherries, dried and chopped
- 1 tablespoon green onions, chopped
- 4 mint leaves, chopped
- 1 cup cherries, pitted and halved

Directions:
In your slow cooker, mix water with farro, stir, cover, and cook on Low for 4 hours, drain and transfer to a bowl. Add salt, oil, lemon juice, vinegar, and dried cherries, fresh cherries, green onions and mint, toss, divide between plates and serve as a side dish.
Enjoy!

Nutrition: calories 162, fat 3, fiber 6, carbs 9, protein 4

Parmesan and Peas Rice

Preparation time: 10 minutes
Cooking time: 2 hours and 30 minutes
Servings: 2

Ingredients:
- 1 cup rice
- 1 tablespoon butter
- 1 small yellow onion, chopped
- ½ tablespoon olive oil
- 1 tablespoon lemon juice
- ½ teaspoon lemon zest, grated
- 1 and ½ cups chicken stock
- 1 tablespoon parsley, chopped
- Salt and black pepper to the taste
- ½ cup peas
- 1 tablespoon parmesan, grated

Directions:
In your slow cooker, mix rice with butter, onion, oil, lemon juice, lemon zest, stock, salt, pepper and peas, stir, cover and cook on High for 2 hours and 30 minutes. Add parmesan, stir until it melts, divide between plates and serve as a side dish.
Enjoy!

Nutrition: calories 162, fat 4, fiber 6, carbs 29, protein 6

Spinach and Cheese Rice

Preparation time: 10 minutes
Cooking time: 2 hours
Servings: 2

Ingredients:
- 1 garlic clove, minced
- 1 tablespoon olive oil
- 1 small yellow onion, chopped
- 1 cup Arborio rice
- 2 tablespoons white wine
- 6 ounces spinach, chopped
- 2 cups veggie stock
- Salt and black pepper to the taste
- 2 ounces goat cheese, crumbled
- 1 tablespoons lemon juice

Directions:
Grease your slow cooker with the oil, add garlic, onion, rice, wine, spinach, stock, salt and pepper, stir, cover and cook on High for 2 hours. Add goat cheese and lemon juice, stir until cheese melts, divide between plates and serve as a side dish.
Enjoy!

Nutrition: calories 300, fat 10, fiber 6, carbs 20, protein 14

Pineapple Rice

Preparation time: 10 minutes
Cooking time: 2 hours
Servings: 2

Ingredients:
- 1 cup rice
- 2 cups water
- 1 small cauliflower, florets separated and chopped
- ½ small pineapple, peeled and chopped
- Salt and black pepper to the taste
- 1 teaspoon olive oil

Directions:
In your slow cooker, mix rice with pineapple, cauliflower, water, oil, salt and pepper, stir, cover and cook on High for 2 hours. Fluff rice mix with a fork, add more salt and pepper to the taste divide between plates and serve as a side dish.
Enjoy

Nutrition: calories 152, fat 4, fiber 5, carbs 18, protein 4

Simple Artichokes

Preparation time: 10 minutes
Cooking time: 3 hours and 30 minutes
Servings: 2

Ingredients:
- 1 cup water
- 2 medium artichokes, trimmed
- 1 tablespoon lemon juice
- Salt to the taste

Directions:
In your slow cooker, mix water with artichokes, salt and lemon juice, stir, cover and cook on Low for 3 hours and 30 minutes. Divide artichokes between plates and serve as a side dish.
 Enjoy!

Nutrition: calories 100, fat 2, fiber 5, carbs 10, protein 4

Simple Bok Choy

Preparation time: 10 minutes
Cooking time: 1 hour and 30 minutes
Servings: 2

Ingredients:
- 3 bok choy bunches, end cut off
- 2 cups water
- 1 garlic clove, minced
- 1 teaspoon ginger, grated
- 1 tablespoon coconut oil
- Salt to the taste

Directions:
Put bok choy in your slow cooker, add the water, cover the pot, cook at High for 1 hour and 30 minutes, transfer to a bowl, add garlic, ginger, oil and salt, toss, divide between plates and serve as a side dish.
Enjoy!

Nutrition: calories 100, fat 1, fiber 2, carbs 7, protein 4

Italian Eggplant Mix

Preparation time: 10 minutes
Cooking time: 2 hours
Servings: 2

Ingredients:
- 2 small eggplants, cubed
- Salt and black pepper to the taste
- 1 tablespoon olive oil
- 1 garlic clove, crushed
- A pinch of hot pepper flakes
- 2 tablespoons oregano, chopped
- ¼ cup water
- 2 anchovies, chopped

Directions:
In your slow cooker, mix eggplants with salt, pepper, oil, garlic, pepper flakes, oregano, water and anchovies, stir, cover and cook on High for 2 hours. Divide between plates and serve as a side dish.
Enjoy!

Nutrition: calories 132, fat 4, fiber 6, carbs 12, protein 3

Slow Cooker Appetizer and Snack Recipes For 2

Artichokes Party Spread

Preparation time: 10 minutes
Cooking time: 2 hours
Servings: 2

Ingredients:
- 2 ounces spinach
- 3 ounces canned artichokes hearts, drained and chopped
- 2 tablespoons mayonnaise
- 2 ounces Alfredo sauce
- A pinch of salt and black pepper
- 1 ounce Swiss cheese, shredded

Directions:
In your slow cooker, mix spinach with artichokes, mayo, Alfredo sauce, salt, pepper and Swiss cheese, stir, cover and cook on Low for 2 hours. Serve as a party spread.
Enjoy!

Nutrition: calories 132, fat 4, fiber 3, carbs 10, protein 4

Caesar Artichoke Dip

Preparation time: 10 minutes
Cooking time: 2 hours
Servings: 2

Ingredients:
- 2 ounces canned artichoke hearts, drained and chopped
- 2 ounces cream cheese, cubed
- 2 tablespoons creamy Caesar dressing
- 1 ounce parmesan, grated
- 2 green onions, chopped
- A pinch of red pepper sauce
- Cooking spray

Directions:
Grease your slow cooker with the cooking spray, add artichokes, cream cheese, Caesar dressing, parmesan, onions and pepper sauce, stir, cover and cook on Low for 2 hours. Divide into bowls and serve as a party dip.
Enjoy!

Nutrition: calories 100, fat 3, fiber 2, carbs 7, protein 3

Crab and Artichoke Spread

Preparation time: 10 minutes
Cooking time: 1 hour and 15 minutes
Servings: 2

Ingredients:
- 2 ounces crabmeat
- 1 teaspoon lemon juice
- 2 tablespoons parmesan, grated
- 2 green onions, chopped
- 2 ounces canned artichokes hearts, drained and chopped
- 2 ounces cream cheese, cubed
- Cooking spray

Directions:
Grease your slow cooker with the spray, add crabmeat, lemon juice, parmesan, onion, artichokes and cream cheese, stir, cover and cook on Low for 1 hour and 15 minutes. Divide into bowls and serve as a party spread.
Enjoy!

Nutrition: calories 100, fat 3, fiber 2, carbs 9, protein 4

Cheesy Crab Dip

Preparation time: 10 minutes
Cooking time: 2 hours
Servings: 2

Ingredients:
- 3 ounces cream cheese, soft
- 3 ounces sour cream
- ½ tablespoon Worcestershire sauce
- 2 tablespoons mayonnaise
- ½ teaspoon mustard
- ½ tablespoon lemon juice
- A pinch of salt and black pepper
- ½ pound crabmeat
- 2 ounces cheddar cheese, shredded
- 1 tablespoon parsley, chopped

Directions:
In your slow cooker, mix cream cheese with sour cream, Worcestershire sauce, mayo, mustard, lemon juice, salt, pepper, crabmeat, cheddar and parsley, stir, cover and cook on Low for 2 hours. Divide into bowls and serve as a dip.
Enjoy!

Nutrition: calories 342, fat 4, fiber 3, carbs 7, protein 10

Squash Spread

Preparation time: 10 minutes
Cooking time: 6 hours
Servings: 2

Ingredients:
- 1 cup butternut squash, peeled and cubed
- 1 tablespoon water
- 2 tablespoons milk
- A pinch of rosemary, dried
- A pinch of sage, dried
- A pinch of salt and black pepper

Directions:
In your slow cooker, mix squash with water, milk, sage, rosemary, salt and pepper, toss, cover and cook on Low for 6 hours. Blend using an immersion blender, divide into bowls and serve as a party spread.
Enjoy!

Nutrition: calories 182, fat 5, fiber 7, carbs 12, protein 5

Cashew Spread

Preparation time: 10 minutes
Cooking time: 7 hours
Servings: 2

Ingredients:
- ¼ cup white beans, dried
- 2 tablespoons cashews, soaked for 12 hours and blended
- ½ teaspoon apple cider vinegar
- ½ cup veggie stock
- ½ tablespoon water

Directions:
In your slow cooker, mix beans with cashews and stock, stir, cover and cook on Low for 6 hours. Drain, transfer to your food processor, add vinegar and water, pulse well, divide into bowls and serve as a party dip
Enjoy!

Nutrition: calories 221, fat 6, fiber 5, carbs 19, protein 3

Veggie Party Rolls

Preparation time: 10 minutes
Cooking time: 8 hours
Servings: 2

Ingredients:
- ½ cup brown lentils, cooked
- ½ green cabbage head, leaves separated
- 1 small onion, chopped
- ½ cup brown rice, already cooked
- 1 ounce white mushrooms, chopped
- 2 tablespoons pine nuts, toasted
- 1 tablespoon raisins
- 1 garlic clove, minced
- 1 tablespoon dill, chopped
- ½ tablespoon olive oil
- 10 ounces marinara sauce
- A pinch of salt and black pepper

Directions:
In a bowl, mix lentils with onion, rice, mushrooms, pine nuts, raisins, garlic, dill, salt and pepper and toss. Arrange cabbage leaves on a working surface, divide lentils mix, wrap them well, add them to your slow cooker, also add marinara sauce, cover and cook on Low for 8 hours. Arrange cabbage rolls on a platter and serve them as an appetizer.
Enjoy!

Nutrition: calories 301, fat 6, fiber 6, carbs 12, protein 3

Veggie Spread

Preparation time: 10 minutes
Cooking time: 7 hours
Servings: 2

Ingredients:
- ½ cup carrots, sliced
- 1 cup cauliflower florets
- 1 tablespoon cashews
- 1 cup water
- ½ cup milk
- ½ teaspoon garlic powder
- ¼ teaspoon smoked paprika
- ¼ teaspoon mustard powder
- A pinch of salt

Directions:
In your slow cooker, mix carrots with cauliflower, cashews and water, stir, cover and cook on Low for 7 hours. Drain, transfer to a blender, add almond milk, garlic powder, paprika, mustard powder and salt, blend well, divide into bowls and serve as a spread.
Enjoy!

Nutrition: calories 301, fat 7, fiber 4, carbs 14, protein 3

Italian Veggie Dip

Preparation time: 10 minutes
Cooking time: 5 hours
Servings: 2

Ingredients:
- ½ small cauliflower head, riced
- 10 ounces canned tomatoes, crushed
- 1 ounce white mushrooms, chopped
- 1 carrot, shredded
- 1 eggplant, cubed
- 2 garlic cloves, minced
- A pinch of salt and black pepper
- 1 tablespoon balsamic vinegar
- 1 tablespoon tomato paste
- ½ tablespoon basil, chopped
- ½ tablespoon oregano, chopped

Directions:
In your slow cooker, mix cauliflower rice with tomatoes, mushrooms, carrots, eggplant, garlic, balsamic vinegar, tomato paste, salt and pepper, stir, cover and cook on High for 5 hours. Add basil and oregano, stir, divide into bowls and serve as a dip.
Enjoy!

Nutrition: calories 261, fat 7, fiber 6, carbs 10, protein 6

Hummus

Preparation time: 10 minutes
Cooking time: 8 hours
Servings: 2

Ingredients:
- ½ cup chickpeas, dried
- 1 tablespoons olive oil
- 1 and ½ cups water
- 1 tablespoon tahini
- A pinch of salt and black pepper
- 1 garlic clove, minced
- ½ tablespoon lemon juice

Directions:
In your slow cooker, mix chickpeas with water, salt and pepper, stir, cover and cook on Low for 8 hours. Drain chickpeas, transfer to a blender, and add oil, tahini, and garlic and lemon juice, blend well, divide into bowls and serve as an appetizer spread.
Enjoy!

Nutrition: calories 211, fat 6, fiber 7, carbs 8, protein 4

Spinach Dip

Preparation time: 10 minutes
Cooking time: 1 hour
Servings: 2

Ingredients:
- 2 tablespoons heavy cream
- ½ cup Greek yogurt
- 5 ounces spinach
- 4 ounces water chestnuts, chopped
- 1 garlic clove, minced
- Salt and black pepper to the taste

Directions:
In your slow cooker, mix cream with spinach, yogurt, chestnuts, salt, black pepper and garlic, stir, cover and cook on High for 30 minutes. Blend using an immersion blender, divide into bowls and serve as a party dip.
Enjoy!

Nutrition: calories 221, fat 5, fiber 7, carbs 12, protein 5

Potato Salad

Preparation time: 10 minutes
Cooking time: 8 hours
Servings: 2

Ingredients:
- 1 small sweet onion, chopped
- 2 tablespoons white vinegar
- 1 tablespoons mustard
- A pinch of salt and black pepper
- 4 gold potatoes, cut into medium chunks
- 1 tablespoon dill, chopped
- ½ cup celery, chopped
- Cooking spray

Directions:
Grease your slow cooker with cooking spray, add onion, vinegar, mustard, salt, pepper, celery and potatoes, toss, cover and cook on Low for 8 hours. Divide salad into bowls, sprinkle dill on top and serve as an appetizer.
Enjoy!

Nutrition: calories 251, fat 6, fiber 7, carbs 8, protein 7

Stuffed Bell Peppers

Preparation time: 10 minutes
Cooking time: 4 hours
Servings: 2

Ingredients:
- 1 small yellow onion, chopped
- 1 teaspoons olive oil
- 1 celery rib, chopped
- ½ tablespoon chili powder
- 1 garlic clove, minced
- 1 teaspoon cumin, ground
- ½ teaspoon oregano, dried
- 1 cup white rice, cooked
- ½ cup corn
- 1 ounce canned pinto beans, drained
- 1 chipotle pepper in adobo
- A pinch of salt and black pepper
- 2 colored bell peppers, tops and insides scooped out
- ½ cup tomato sauce

Directions:
Heat up a pan with the oil over medium-high heat, add onion, celery and garlic, stir, cook for 3-4 minutes, take off heat, mix with chili, cumin, oregano, rice, corn, beans, salt, pepper and chipotle pepper and stir well. Stuff bell peppers with this mix, put them in your slow cooker, add tomato sauce, cover, cook on Low for 4 hours, transfer peppers on a platter and serve as an appetizer. Enjoy!

Nutrition: calories 253, fat 5, fiber 4, carbs 12, protein 3

Corn Dip

Preparation time: 10 minutes
Cooking time: 2 hours
Servings: 2

Ingredients:
- 6 ounces canned corn, drained
- 2 green onions, chopped
- 2 tablespoons heavy cream
- 2 ounces cream cheese, cubed
- 1 jalapeno, chopped
- ¼ teaspoon chili powder

Directions:
In your slow cooker, mix corn with green onions, cream, cheese, chili powder and jalapeno, whisk well, cover and cook on Low for 2 hours. Divide into bowls and serve as a dip. Enjoy!

Nutrition: calories 272, fat 5, fiber 10, carbs 12, protein 4

Cheesy Mushroom Salsa

Preparation time: 10 minutes
Cooking time: 4 hours
Servings: 2

Ingredients:
- 1 cup green bell peppers, chopped
- 1 small yellow onion, chopped
- 1 garlic clove, minced
- ½ pound mushrooms, chopped
- 12 ounces tomato sauce
- ¼ cup cream cheese, cubed
- Salt and black pepper to the taste

Directions:
In your slow cooker, mix bell peppers with onion, garlic, mushrooms, tomato sauce, cheese, salt and pepper, stir, cover and cook on Low for 4 hours. Divide into bowls and serve as a party salsa with crackers on the side.
Enjoy!

Nutrition: calories 285, fat 4, fiber 7, carbs 12, protein 4

Refried Beans Spread

Preparation time: 10 minutes
Cooking time: 1 hour
Servings: 2

Ingredients:
- ¼ cup salsa
- 1 cup canned refried beans
- ½ cup nacho cheese
- 1 tablespoon green onions, chopped

Directions:
In your slow cooker, mix refried beans with salsa, nacho cheese and green onions, stir, cover and cook on High for 1 hour. Divide into bowls and serve as a party dip
Enjoy!

Nutrition: calories 302, fat 5, fiber 10, carbs 16, protein 6

Thai Tofu Party Mix

Preparation time: 10 minutes
Cooking time: 10 hours
Servings: 2

Ingredients:
- 1 pound firm tofu, pressed and cut into rectangles
- ½ tablespoons sesame oil
- 1 tablespoon soy sauce
- ¼ cup veggie stock
- ½ cup pineapple juice
- 2 tablespoons rice vinegar
- 1 tablespoon sugar
- ½ tablespoon ginger, grated
- 1 garlic clove, minced
- 3 pineapple rings

Directions:
In your slow cooker, mix tofu with sesame oil, soy sauce, stock, pineapple juice, vinegar, sugar, ginger, garlic and pineapple rings, stir, cover and cook on Low for 10 hours. Divide into bowls and serve as an appetizer.
Enjoy!

Nutrition: calories 201, fat 5, fiber 7, carbs 15, protein 4

Chickpeas Appetizer Salad

Preparation time: 10 minutes
Cooking time: 12 hours
Servings: 2

Ingredients:
- 1 cup chickpeas
- 2 cups water
- 1 small yellow onion, chopped
- ¼ tablespoon ginger, grated
- 4 garlic cloves, minced
- 2 Thai peppers, chopped
- ¼ tablespoons cumin, ground
- ¼ tablespoons coriander, ground
- ¼ tablespoons red chili powder
- ¼ tablespoons garam masala
- ¼ tablespoon tamarind paste
- 1 tablespoon lemon juice

Directions:
In your slow cooker, mix chickpeas with water, stir, cover and cook on Low for 10 hours. In your blender, mix onion with ginger, garlic, Thai peppers, cumin, coriander, chili powder, garam masala, tamarind paste and lemon juice, pulse well, add this to slow cooker, toss, well, cover and cook on Low for 2 hours more. Divide into bowls and serve as an appetizer.
Enjoy!

Nutrition: calories 355, fat 5, fiber 14, carbs 16, protein 11

Creamy Mushroom Appetizer

Preparation time: 10 minutes
Cooking time: 4 hours
Servings: 2

Ingredients:
- 1 pound mushroom caps
- 1 yellow onion, chopped
- 3 garlic cloves, minced
- 1 cup veggie stock
- 1 tablespoon heavy cream
- 2 teaspoons smoked paprika
- Salt and black pepper to the taste
- 2 tablespoons parsley, chopped

Directions:
In your slow cooker, mix mushrooms with garlic, onion, stock and paprika, stir, cover and cook on High for 4 hours. Add parsley, coconut cream, salt and pepper, toss, arrange on a platter and serve them as an appetizer.
Enjoy!

Nutrition: calories 300, fat 6, fiber 12, carbs 16, protein 6

Bulgur Appetizer Salad

Preparation time: 10 minutes
Cooking time: 8 hours
Servings: 2

Ingredients:
- 1 cup white mushrooms, sliced
- ½ cup bulgur
- 1 small yellow onion, chopped
- 1 small red bell pepper, chopped
- ½ cup veggie stock
- 1 garlic clove, minced
- 1 cup strong coffee
- 5 ounces canned kidney beans, drained
- 1 tablespoon sugar
- 1 tablespoon chili powder
- ½ tablespoon cocoa powder
- ¼ teaspoon oregano, dried
- Salt and black pepper to the taste

Directions:
In your slow cooker, mix mushrooms with bulgur, onion, bell pepper, stock, garlic, coffee, kidney, sugar, chili powder, cocoa, oregano, salt and pepper, stir gently, cover and cook on Low for 12 hours. Divide into bowls and serve cold as an appetizer.
Enjoy!

Nutrition: calories 351, fat 4, fiber 6, carbs 12, protein 4

Root Veggie Salad

Preparation time: 10 minutes
Cooking time: 6 hours
Servings: 2

Ingredients:
- ½ cup turnips, cubed
- ½ cup rutabagas, cubed
- ½ cup sweet potatoes, cubed
- ½ cup parsnips, cubed
- ¼ cup beets, cubed
- ¼ cup carrots, cubed
- 1 small yellow onion, chopped
- 2 ounces tempeh, rinsed and cubed
- 5 ounces canned tomatoes, chopped
- ¼ cup veggie stock
- 3 ounces canned black beans, drained
- Salt and black pepper to the taste
- ½ teaspoon nutmeg, ground
- ½ teaspoon sweet paprika
- ½ cup parsley, chopped

Directions:
In your slow cooker, mix turnips with rutabagas, potatoes, parsnips, beets, carrots, onion, tempeh, tomatoes, stock, black beans, salt, pepper, nutmeg and paprika, stir, cover and cook on Low for 6 hours. Add parsley, stir, divide into bowls and serve cold as an appetizer.
Enjoy!

Nutrition: calories 300, fat 6, fiber 6, carbs 16, protein 6

Lentils Sloppy Joe

Preparation time: 10 minutes
Cooking time: 1 hour and 30 minutes
Servings: 2

Ingredients:
- ¼ cup blackstrap molasses
- 10 ounces canned tomatoes, crushed
- 3 ounces tomato paste
- 2 tablespoons white vinegar
- 1 tablespoon apple cider vinegar
- 1 small sweet onion, chopped
- 1 garlic clove, minced
- ½ teaspoon dry mustard
- ½ tablespoon sugar
- A pinch of red pepper flakes
- A pinch of salt and black pepper
- 1/8 teaspoon liquid smoke
- 2 cups green lentils, cooked and drained
- 2 buns for serving

Directions:
Put molasses in your slow cooker; add tomatoes, tomato paste, vinegar, apple cider vinegar, onion, garlic, mustard, sugar, salt, pepper flakes, cayenne and liquid smoke. Stir, cover and cook on High for 1 hour and 30 minutes. Add lentils, stir gently, divide into 2 buns and serve as a snack.
Enjoy!

Nutrition: calories 260, fat 3, fiber 4, carbs 6, protein 7

Easy and Tasty Tacos

Preparation time: 10 minutes
Cooking time: 4 hours
Servings: 2

Ingredients:
- 13 ounces canned pinto beans, drained
- ¼ cup chili sauce
- 2 ounces chipotle pepper in adobo sauce, chopped
- ½ cup corn
- 2 ounces tomato paste
- ½ tablespoon cocoa powder
- ¼ teaspoon cinnamon, ground
- ¼ teaspoon cumin, ground
- 4 taco shells

Directions:
Put the beans in your slow cooker; add chili sauce, chipotle pepper, corn, tomato paste, cocoa powder, cinnamon and cumin. Stir, cover and cook on Low for 4 hours. Divide beans mix into taco shells and serve them as an appetizer.
Enjoy!

Nutrition: calories 352, fat 3, fiber 6, carbs 12, protein 10

Almond Snack

Preparation time: 10 minutes
Cooking time: 4 hours
Servings: 2

Ingredients:
- 1 tablespoon cinnamon powder
- 1 cup sugar
- 1 and ½ cups almonds
- 2 tablespoons water
- ½ teaspoons vanilla extract

Directions:
In a bowl, mix water with vanilla extract and whisk. In another bowl, mix cinnamon with sugar and stir. Dip almonds in water, then in cinnamon and sugar mix, toss well, transfer them to your slow cooker, cover and cook on Low for 4 hours. Divide into bowls and serve as a snack.
Enjoy!

Nutrition: calories 260, fat 3, fiber 4, carbs 12, protein 8

Eggplant Salsa

Preparation time: 10 minutes
Cooking time: 7 hours
Servings: 2

Ingredients:
- 1 cup tomatoes, chopped
- 1 and ½ cups eggplant, chopped
- 1 teaspoon capers
- 2 garlic cloves, minced
- ½ tablespoon basil, chopped
- 1 teaspoon balsamic vinegar
- A pinch of salt and black pepper
- 2 ounces green olives, pitted and sliced

Directions:
Put tomatoes and eggplants in your slow cooker; add garlic, capers, basil and olives, stir, cover and cook on Low for 7 hours. Add salt, pepper, vinegar, stir gently, divide into small bowls and serve as an appetizer.
Enjoy!

Nutrition: calories 170, fat 3, fiber 5, carbs 10, protein 5

Almond and Beans Spread

Preparation time: 10 minutes
Cooking time: 8 hours
Servings: 2

Ingredients:
- ¼ cup almonds
- 1 cup water
- ½ teaspoon nutritional yeast flakes
- 2 tablespoons great northern beans
- A pinch of salt and black pepper

Directions:
Put the water in your slow cooker, add almonds and beans, stir, cover and cook on Low for 8 hours. Transfer these to your blender, add yeast flakes, salt and black pepper, pulse really well, divide into bowls and serve as a party spread.
Enjoy!

Nutrition: calories 270, fat 4, fiber 4, carbs 8, protein 10

Onion Dip

Preparation time: 10 minutes
Cooking time: 8 hours
Servings: 2

Ingredients:
- 1 and ½ cups yellow onions, chopped
- A pinch of salt and black pepper
- 1 tablespoon olive oil
- ½ tablespoon butter
- ½ cup milk
- 2 tablespoons mayonnaise

Directions:
Put the onions in your slow cooker, add salt, pepper oil and butter, stir well, cover and cook on High for 8 hours. Drain excess liquid, transfer onion to a bowl, add milk and mayonnaise, whisk well and serve as a party dip.
Enjoy!

Nutrition: calories 240, fat 4, fiber 4, carbs 9, protein 7

Simple Nuts Snack

Preparation time: 10 minutes
Cooking time: 2 hours
Servings: 2

Ingredients:
- 2 tablespoons almonds, toasted
- 2 tablespoons cashews
- 2 tablespoons pecans, halved and toasted
- 2 tablespoons hazelnuts, toasted and peeled
- 2 tablespoons sugar
- ¼ teaspoon ginger, grated
- 2 tablespoons butter, melted
- A pinch of cinnamon powder
- A pinch of cloves, ground
- A pinch of cayenne pepper

Directions:
Put almonds, pecans, cashews and hazelnuts in your slow cooker, add sugar, butter, ginger, cayenne, cloves and cinnamon, stir, cover, cook on Low for 2 hours, divide into bowls and serve as a snack.
Enjoy!

Nutrition: calories 125, fat 3, fiber 2, carbs 5, protein 5

Eggplant Appetizer Salad

Preparation time: 10 minutes
Cooking time: 8 hours
Servings: 2

Ingredients:
- 1 small eggplant, cut into quarters and then sliced
- 10 ounces canned plum tomatoes
- 1 red bell pepper, chopped
- ½ red onion, sliced
- 1 teaspoon cumin, ground
- A pinch of salt and black pepper
- 1 teaspoon sweet paprika
- 1 tablespoon lemon juice

Directions:
In your slow cooker, mix eggplant with tomatoes, bell pepper, onion, cumin, salt, pepper, paprika and lemon juice, stir, cover, cook on Low for 8 hours, divide into bowls and serve cold as an appetizer salad.
Enjoy!

Nutrition: calories 203, fat 2, fiber 3, carbs 7, protein 8

Lentils Dip

Preparation time: 10 minutes
Cooking time: 6 hours
Servings: 2

Ingredients:
- 1 small yellow bell pepper, chopped
- 1 small yellow onion, chopped
- 2 carrots, chopped
- 2 garlic cloves, minced
- A pinch of cayenne pepper
- 1 cup veggie stock
- 1 and ½ cups red lentils, dried
- A pinch of sea salt
- ½ tablespoon rosemary, chopped
- 1 tablespoon lemon zest, grated
- 1 tablespoon lemon juice

Directions:
Put the stock in your slow cooker; add bell pepper, onion, carrots, garlic, lentils, cayenne and salt, stir, cover and cook on Low for 6 hours. Add rosemary, lemon zest and juice, stir, divide into bowls and serve as a party dip.
Enjoy!

Nutrition: calories 200, fat 2, fiber 5, carbs 8, protein 6

Beef Party Meatballs

Preparation time: 10 minutes
Cooking time: 8 hours
Servings: 2

Ingredients:
- 1 pound beef, ground
- 1 egg, whisked
- 7 ounces canned tomatoes, crushed
- 6 ounces canned tomato puree
- 2 tablespoons parsley, chopped
- 1 garlic clove, minced
- 1 small yellow onion, chopped
- Black pepper to the taste

Directions:
In a bowl, mix beef with egg, parsley, garlic, black pepper and onion, stir well, shape small meatballs, place them in your slow cooker add tomato puree and crushed tomatoes on top, cover and cook on Low for 8 hours. Arrange them on a platter and serve as an appetizer.
Enjoy!

Nutrition: calories 170, fat 5, fiber 3, carbs 10, protein 7

Stuffed Jalapenos

Preparation time: 10 minutes
Cooking time: 3 hours
Servings: 2

Ingredients:
- ¼ pound chorizo, chopped
- 4 jalapenos, tops cut off and deseeded
- 1 small white onion, chopped
- ¼ pound beef, ground
- ¼ teaspoon garlic powder
- ½ tablespoon maple syrup
- ½ tablespoon mustard
- ¼ cup water

Directions:
In a bowl, mix beef with chorizo, garlic powder and onion, stir, stuff your jalapenos with the mix, put them in your slow cooker, add the water, cover and cook on High for 3 hours. In a bowl, mix maple syrup with mustard and whisk well. Brush jalapenos with this mix, arrange on a platter and serve as an appetizer.
Enjoy!

Nutrition: calories 170, fat 2, fiber 3, carbs 8, protein 3

Fish Sticks

Preparation time: 10 minutes
Cooking time: 2 hours
Servings: 2

Ingredients:
- 1 eggs, whisked
- ½ pound cod fillets, cut into medium strips
- ½ cup flour
- A pinch of salt and black pepper
- ¼ teaspoon sweet paprika
- Cooking spray

Directions:
In a bowl, mix flour with salt, pepper and paprika and stir. Put the egg in another bowl and whisk it. Dip fish sticks in the egg and then dredge them in flour mix. Grease your slow cooker with cooking spray, add fish sticks, cover, cook on High for 2 hours, arrange on a platter and serve as an appetizer.
Enjoy!

Nutrition: calories 200, fat 2, fiber 4, carbs 13, protein 12

Easy Pecans Snack

Preparation time: 10 minutes
Cooking time: 2 hours
Servings: 2

Ingredients:
- ½ pound pecans, halved
- 1 tablespoon olive oil
- ½ teaspoon basil, dried
- ½ tablespoon chili powder
- ½ teaspoon oregano, dried
- ½ teaspoon thyme, dried
- ½ teaspoon onion powder

Directions:
In your slow cooker, mix pecans with oil, basil, chili powder, oregano, onion powder and thyme, toss to coat, cover, cook on Low for 2 hours, divide into bowls and serve as a snack.
Enjoy!

Nutrition: calories 108, fat 3, fiber 2, carbs 9, protein 2

Sausage Bites

Preparation time: 10 minutes
Cooking time: 4 hours
Servings: 2

Ingredients:
- 2 pork sausages, sliced
- 1 ounce chili sauce
- 2 tablespoons grape jelly

Directions:
Put sausage slices in your slow cooker, add chili sauce and grape jelly, toss well, cover and cook on Low for 4 hours. Serve them as an appetizer or snack.
Enjoy!

Nutrition: calories 200, fat 6, fiber 3, carbs 15, protein 12

Spinach Spread

Preparation time: 10 minutes
Cooking time: 2 hours
Servings: 2

Ingredients:
- ½ cup milk
- ½ cup cashews
- 1 tablespoons lemon juice
- 1 garlic clove, chopped
- 1 teaspoon mustard
- 1 tablespoon mayonnaise
- 8 ounces spinach
- Black pepper to the taste

Directions:
In your food processor, mix cashews with garlic, milk, mustard and lemon juice, blend well, transfer this to your slow cooker, and add spinach, mayo and black pepper, stir, cover and cook on High for 2 hours. Divide into bowls and serve as a party spread.
Enjoy!

Nutrition: calories 260, fat 4, fiber 2, carbs 12, protein 5

Beef Cakes

Preparation time: 10 minutes
Cooking time: 4 hours
Servings: 2

Ingredients:
- ½ pound beef
- 1 small yellow onion, chopped
- 1 egg
- A pinch of salt and black pepper to the taste
- 1 tablespoon cilantro, chopped
- 5 ounces coconut milk
- 1 tablespoon hot sauce
- ½ teaspoon basil, dried
- ¼ tablespoon green curry paste
- ½ tablespoon soy sauce

Directions:
Put the meat in a bowl, add onion, egg, salt, pepper and cilantro, stir well, shape medium sized cakes and place them in your slow cooker. Add hot sauce, soy sauce, coconut milk, curry paste and basil, toss and cook on Low for 4 hours. Arrange meatballs on a platter and serve them as an appetizer
Enjoy!

Nutrition: calories 225, fat 6, fiber 2, carbs 8, protein 4

Squid Appetizer

Preparation time: 10 minutes
Cooking time: 7 hours
Servings: 2

Ingredients:
- ½ pound squid, cleaned and cut into rings
- 1 tablespoon sugar
- 1 small ginger piece, grated
- 2 garlic cloves, minced
- 1 tablespoon soy sauce
- 1 cup veggie stock
- 1 leek stalks, chopped
- 1 bay leaf

Directions:
Put the squid in your slow cooker; add sugar, ginger, garlic, soy sauce, leeks, stock, black pepper and bay leaf, stir, cover and cook on Low for 8 hours. Divide into bowls and serve right away as an appetizer.
Enjoy!

Nutrition: calories 230, fat 2, fiber 4, carbs 7, protein 5

Seafood Salad

Preparation time: 10 minutes
Cooking time: 5 hours
Servings: 2

Ingredients:
- ½ pound shrimp, peeled and deveined
- 1 small yellow onions, chopped
- 1 celery stalk, chopped
- 1 red bell pepper, chopped
- 1 green onion, chopped
- 1 tablespoon olive oil
- ½ tablespoon flour
- 1 garlic clove, minced
- 2 ounces canned tomatoes and chilies, chopped
- ½ pound crawfish tails, cooked and peeled
- ¼ cup water
- 1 ounce tomato paste
- ¼ teaspoon oregano, dried
- ¼ teaspoon basil, dried
- A pinch of red pepper, crushed
- 1 tablespoon parsley, chopped

Directions:
Heat up a pan with the oil over medium-high heat, add onions, bell pepper, celery and green onions, stir and cook for a couple of minutes. Add garlic and tomatoes, stir, transfer everything to your slow cooker, and add tomato paste, water, flour, black pepper, oregano, basil, red pepper and parsley, stir, cover and cook on Low for 4 hours. Add shrimp and crawfish, stir, cover and cook on Low for 1 more hour. Divide into bowls and serve warm or cold as an appetizer.
Enjoy!

Nutrition: calories 240, fat 2, fiber 5, carbs 7, protein 2

Stuffed Chicken Appetizer

Preparation time: 10 minutes
Cooking time: 6 hours
Servings: 2

Ingredients:
- 2 chicken breasts, skinless and boneless
- ½ tablespoon olive oil
- 1 small yellow onion, chopped
- 1 chili pepper, chopped
- 1 small red bell pepper, chopped
- 1 teaspoons garlic, minced
- 2 ounces spinach
- 1 teaspoon oregano, chopped
- ½ tablespoon lemon juice
- ½ cup veggie stock
- A pinch of salt and black pepper

Directions:
Heat up a pan with the oil over medium-high heat, add bell pepper, chili peppers, onions, spinach, garlic, salt, pepper and oregano, stir, cook for 4 minutes and take off heat. Cut a pocket in the chicken breasts, stuff them with spinach mix, place them in your slow cooker, add stock, cover and cook on Low for 6 hours. Arrange on a platter, drizzle the lemon juice and serve as an appetizer.
Enjoy!

Nutrition: calories 245, fat 4, fiber 3, carbs 10, protein 6

Apple Dip

Preparation time: 10 minutes
Cooking time: 8 hours
Servings: 2

Ingredients:
- 2 cups apples, peeled, cored and chopped
- ¼ teaspoon allspice, ground
- ¼ teaspoon clove, ground
- ¼ teaspoon ginger powder
- 1 tablespoon lemon juice
- 2 teaspoons cinnamon powder
- ¼ teaspoon nutmeg, ground
- ½ cup water
- 2 tablespoons maple syrup

Directions:
In your slow cooker, mix apples with allspice, clove, ginger, cinnamon, nutmeg, maple syrup, water and lemon juice, stir, cover and cook on Low for 8 hours. Blend using an immersion blender, divide into bowls and serve as a sweet dip.
Enjoy!

Nutrition: calories 212, fat 4, fiber 6, carbs 12, protein 3

Sweet Potato Dip

Preparation time: 10 minutes
Cooking time: 4 hours
Servings: 2

Ingredients:
- 2 sweet potatoes, pricked with a fork
- ¼ cup walnuts
- 1 garlic clove
- 1 cup basil leaves
- 2 tablespoons olive oil
- 1 tablespoon lemon juice
- A pinch of salt and black pepper

Directions:
Wrap sweet potatoes in tin foil, add them to your slow cooker, cover, cook on High for 4hours, transfer them to a cutting board, unwrap, cool them down, peel and mash them with a fork. In a blender, mix walnuts with garlic, basil, oil, salt, pepper and lemon juice and pulse really well. Mix sweet potato mash with basil pesto, stir well, divide into bowls and serve as a dip.
Enjoy!

Nutrition: calories 253, fat 5, fiber 6, carbs 13, protein 4

Squash Salad

Preparation time: 10 minutes
Cooking time: 4 hours
Servings: 2

Ingredients:
- 1 butternut squash, peeled and cubed
- 1 small yellow onion, chopped
- ½ teaspoons thyme, chopped
- 1 garlic cloves, minced
- A pinch of salt and black pepper
- 2 ounces veggie stock
- 1 ounce baby spinach

Directions:
In your slow cooker, mix squash with onion, thyme, salt, pepper and stock, stir, cover, cook on Low for 4 hours, transfer to a bowl, add spinach, toss and serve as an appetizer salad.
Enjoy!

Nutrition: calories 160, fat 1, fiber 4, carbs 18, protein 4

Chicken Meatballs

Preparation time: 10 minutes
Cooking time: 7 hours
Servings: 2

Ingredients:
- 6 ounces canned tomatoes, crushed
- 1 small yellow onion, halved
- 1 garlic clove, minced
- 1 tablespoon tomato paste
- ½ tablespoons olive oil
- 1 bay leaf
- 1 basil spring, chopped
- A pinch of red pepper flakes, crushed

For the meatballs:
- ½ pound chicken, ground
- 1 tablespoon milk
- 1 egg
- 1 teaspoon oregano, dried
- 1 tablespoon parsley, chopped
- A pinch of salt and black pepper

Directions:
In your slow cooker, mix tomatoes with onion, garlic, tomato paste, olive oil, bay leaf, basil and pepper flakes, stir, cover and cook on Low for 6 hours. In a bowl, mix chicken with milk, egg, oregano, parsley, salt and pepper, stir well, shape medium meatballs, add them to your slow cooker, cover and cook on High for 1 hour. Arrange meatballs on a platter drizzle sauce all over and serve them as an appetizer.
Enjoy!

Nutrition: calories 201, fat 4, fiber 5, carbs 8, protein 2

Pecans Snack

Preparation time: 10 minutes
Cooking time: 3 hours
Servings: 2

Ingredients:
- ½ cup sugar
- ½ tablespoon cinnamon powder
- 1 egg white
- 1 teaspoon vanilla extract
- 2 cups pecans
- 2 tablespoons water
- Cooking spray

Directions:
In a bowl, mix sugar with cinnamon, egg white with vanilla and whisk well. Grease your slow cooker with cooking spray, add pecans, cinnamon and egg white mix, toss, cover and cook on Low for 3 hours. Divide pecans into bowls and serve as a snack.
Enjoy!

Nutrition: calories 172, fat 3, fiber 5, carbs 8, protein 2

Seasoned Peanuts

Preparation time: 10 minutes
Cooking time: 8 hours
Servings: 2

Ingredients:
- ½ pounds green peanuts
- 1 cup water
- A pinch of sea salt
- ½ tablespoon Cajun seasoning

Directions:
In your slow cooker, mix peanuts with water, salt and Cajun seasoning, stir, cover, cook on Low for 8 hours, drain, transfer to bowls and serve as a snack.
Enjoy!

Nutrition: calories 100, fat 2, fiber 3, carbs 7, protein 3

Cauliflower Dip

Preparation time: 10 minutes
Cooking time: 2 hours
Servings: 2

Ingredients:
- 2 bacon slices, chopped and cooked
- 1 jalapeno, chopped
- 2 tablespoons heavy cream
- 1 cup cauliflower rice
- 2 tablespoons cream cheese, cubed
- A pinch of salt and black pepper
- 1 tablespoon chives, chopped

Directions:
In your slow cooker, mix bacon with jalapenos, cream, cauliflower, salt and pepper, stir, cover and cook on Low for 2 hours. Add cream cheese and chives, stir well, leave aside for a few minutes, divide into bowls and serve as a dip.
Enjoy!

Nutrition: calories 202, fat 3, fiber 3, carbs 7, protein 6

Walnuts and Pumpkin Seeds Snack

Preparation time: 10 minutes
Cooking time: 2 hours and 30 minutes
Servings: 2

Ingredients:
- Cooking spray
- 3 tablespoons walnuts, chopped
- 3 tablespoons pumpkin seeds
- 1 tablespoon dill, dried
- ½ tablespoons olive oil
- 1 teaspoon rosemary, dried
- 1 tablespoon lemon peel, shredded

Directions:
Grease your slow cooker with cooking spray, add walnuts, pumpkin seeds, oil, dill, rosemary and lemon peel, toss, cover and cook on Low for 2 hours and 30 minutes. Divide into bowls and serve them as a snack.
Enjoy!

Nutrition: calories 100, fat 2, fiber 2, carbs 3, protein 2

Mini Sausages Snack

Preparation time: 10 minutes
Cooking time: 4 hours
Servings: 2

Ingredients:
- 6 mini smoked sausages
- 2 tablespoons tomato sauce
- 1 teaspoon sweet paprika
- ½ cup grape juice

Directions:
In your slow cooker, mix pork sausages with tomato sauce, paprika and grape juice, stir well, cover and cook on Low for 4 hours. Arrange mini sausages on plates and serve as a snack.
Enjoy!

Nutrition: calories 251, fat 4, fiber 6, carbs 7, protein 3

Chicken Dip

Preparation time: 10 minutes
Cooking time: 3 hours and 30 minutes
Servings: 2

Ingredients:
- ½ pound chicken breast, skinless, boneless and sliced
- 1 tablespoon sriracha sauce
- 3 tablespoons chicken stock
- ½ tablespoons sugar
- 1 teaspoon hot sauce
- 3 ounces heavy cream

Directions:
In your slow cooker, mix chicken with sriracha sauce, stock, sugar and hot sauce, stir, cover and cook on High for 3 hours. Shred meat, return to pot, also add cream, cover, cook on High for 30 minutes more, divide into bowls and serve as a party dip.
Enjoy!

Nutrition: calories 301, fat 3, fiber 6, carbs 11, protein 5

Slow Cooker Dessert Recipes For 2

Stuffed Apples

Preparation time: 10 minutes
Cooking time: 1 hour and 30 minutes
Servings: 2

Ingredients:
- 2 tablespoons maple syrup
- 2 tablespoons figs, dried
- ½ teaspoon sugar
- 2 tablespoons pecans, chopped
- ½ teaspoon lemon zest, grated
- ½ teaspoon orange zest, grated
- ½ teaspoon cinnamon powder
- A pinch of nutmeg, ground
- ½ tablespoon lemon juice
- ½ tablespoon olive oil
- ¼ cup water
- 2 apples, cored and tops cut off

Directions:
In a bowl, mix maple syrup with figs, sugar, pecans, lemon zest, orange zest, ½ teaspoon cinnamon, nutmeg, lemon juice and coconut oil, whisk really well and stuff apples with this mix. Add the water to your slow cooker, add the rest of the cinnamon and the apples, cover and cook on High for 1 hour and 30 minutes. Divide apples between plates and serve them for breakfast. Enjoy!

Nutrition: calories 189, fat 4, fiber 7, carbs 19, protein 2

Sweet Apples and Cane Juice

Preparation time: 10 minutes
Cooking time: 4 hours
Servings: 2

Ingredients:
- 2 tablespoons coconut oil, melted
- ½ tablespoon lemon juice
- 3 tablespoons cane juice, evaporated
- ¼ teaspoon cinnamon powder
- ½ teaspoon vanilla extract
- 2 apples, cored, peeled and cubed

Directions:
In your slow cooker mix oil with cane juice, lemon juice, cinnamon and vanilla and whisk well. Add apple, toss well, cover, cook on High for 4 hours, divide into bowls and serve.
Enjoy!

Nutrition: calories 200, fat 4, fiber 6, carbs 16, protein 3

Banana Cake

Preparation time: 10 minutes
Cooking time: 2 hours
Servings: 2

Ingredients:
- ½ cup sugar
- 2 tablespoons butter, soft
- ½ teaspoon vanilla
- 1 egg
- 2 bananas, mashed
- ½ teaspoon baking powder
- 1 cup flour
- ¼ teaspoons baking soda
- ¼ cup milk
- Cooking spray

Directions:
In a bowl, mix butter with sugar, vanilla extract, eggs, mashed bananas, baking powder, flour, baking soda and milk and whisk. Grease your slow cooker with cooking spray, add cake batter, spread, cover and cook on High for 2 hours. Leave cake to cool down, slice and serve.
Enjoy!

Nutrition: calories 300, fat 4, fiber 4, carbs 27, protein 4

Coconut and Chocolate Cream

Preparation time: 10 minutes
Cooking time: 1 hour
Servings: 2

Ingredients:
- 2 ounces coconut cream
- 2 ounces dark chocolate, cut into chunks
- ½ teaspoon sugar

Directions:
In a bowl, mix coconut cream with chocolate and sugar, whisk well, pour into your slow cooker, cover, cook on High for 1 hour, divide into bowls and serve cold.
Enjoy!

Nutrition: calories 242, fat 12, fiber 6, carbs 9, protein 4

Winter Pudding

Preparation time: 10 minutes
Cooking time: 1 hour
Servings: 2

Ingredients:
- ½ cup almond milk
- ¼ cup pumpkin puree
- 1 tablespoons maple syrup
- ¼ cup milk
- 2 tablespoons chia seeds
- ¼ teaspoon cinnamon powder
- ¼ teaspoon ginger, grated

Directions:
In your slow cooker, mix almond milk with milk, pumpkin, maple syrup, chia, cinnamon and ginger, stir, cover and cook on High for 1 hour. Divide pudding into bowls and serve cold
Enjoy!

Nutrition: calories 205, fat 2, fiber 7, carbs 11, protein 4

Cherry and Cocoa Compote

Preparation time: 10 minutes
Cooking time: 2 hours
Servings: 2

Ingredients:
- ¼ cup cocoa powder
- ½ cup red cherry juice
- 2 tablespoons maple syrup
- ½ pound cherries, pitted and halved
- 1 tablespoons sugar
- 1cups water

Directions:
In your slow cooker, mix cocoa with cherry juice, maple syrup, cherries, water and sugar, stir, cover, cook on High for 2 hours, divide into bowls and serve cold.
Enjoy!

Nutrition: calories 200, fat 1, fiber 4, carbs 5, protein 2

Berry and Cashew Cake

Preparation time: 10 minutes
Cooking time: 2 hours
Servings: 2

Ingredients:
For the base:
- ¼ cup dates, pitted
- ½ tablespoon water
- ¼ teaspoon vanilla
- ¼ cup almonds

For the cake:

- 1 and ½ cups cashews, soaked for 8 hours
- ½ cup blueberries
- ½ cup maple syrup
- ½ tablespoon vegetable oil

Directions:
In your food processor, mix dates with water, vanilla and almonds, pulse well, transfer it to a working surface, flatten and arrange it on the bottom of your slow cooker. In your blender, mix maple syrup with coconut oil, cashews and blueberries, blend well, spread over crust, cover and cook on High for 2 hours. Leave cake to cool down, slice and serve.
Enjoy!

Nutrition: calories 200, fat 3, fiber 5, carbs 12, protein 3

Cashew and Coconut Pudding

Preparation time: 10 minutes
Cooking time: 1 hour
Servings: 2

Ingredients:
- ¼ cup cashew butter
- 1 tablespoon vegetable oil
- 2 tablespoons coconut butter
- 2 tablespoons lemon juice
- ½ teaspoon lemon zest, grated
- ½ tablespoons maple syrup

Directions:
In a bowl, mix cashew butter with coconut butter, oil, lemon juice, lemon zest and maple syrup and stir until you obtain a creamy mix. Pour into your slow cooker, cook on High for 1 hour, divide into bowls and serve.
Enjoy!

Nutrition: calories 202, fat 4, fiber 5, carbs 14, protein 1

Simple Citrus Pudding

Preparation time: 10 minutes
Cooking time: 1 hour
Servings: 2

Ingredients:
- ½ teaspoon baking powder
- ½ cup flour
- 1 tablespoon sugar
- ½ teaspoon cinnamon powder
- 1 and ½ tablespoons vegetable oil
- ¼ cup milk
- 2 tablespoons pecans, chopped
- 2 tablespoons raisins
- 2 tablespoons orange peel, grated
- ½ cup orange juice

Directions:
In a bowl, mix flour with sugar, baking powder, cinnamon, half of the oil, milk, pecans and raisins, stir and pour into your slow cooker. In a pan, mix orange juice, orange peel and the rest of the oil, stir, bring to a boil over medium heat and pour over the pudding Cover, cook on High for 1 hour, leave aside to cool down, slice and serve.
Enjoy!

Nutrition: calories 252, fat 3, fiber 3, carbs 7, protein 3

Creamy Apples

Preparation time: 10 minutes
Cooking time: 1 hour
Servings: 2

Ingredients:
- ½ teaspoon cinnamon powder
- 3 ounces apples, cored and chopped
- 1 egg, whisked
- ¼ cup whipping cream
- 1 tablespoon sugar
- ½ teaspoon nutmeg, ground
- 1 teaspoons vanilla extract
- 2 tablespoons pecans, chopped

Directions:
In your slow cooker, mix cream, vanilla, nutmeg, sugar, apples, egg and cinnamon, stir, cover, cook on High for 1 hour, divide into bowls, sprinkle pecans on top and serve cold
Enjoy!

Nutrition: calories 260, fat 3, fiber 2, carbs 14, protein 3

Cinnamon Plum Compote

Preparation time: 10 minutes
Cooking time: 1 hour
Servings: 2

Ingredients:
- 1 pound plums, stones removed and chopped
- ½ cup water
- 1 tablespoon sugar
- 1 teaspoon cinnamon powder

Directions:
Put plums, water, stevia and cinnamon in your slow cooker, cover and cook on High for 1 hour. Divide bowls and serve cold.
Enjoy!

Nutrition: calories 203, fat 0, fiber 1, carbs 5, protein 4

Apple Cake

Preparation time: 10 minutes
Cooking time: 2 hours and 30 minutes
Servings: 2

Ingredients:
- 1 and ½ cups apples, cored and cubed
- 1 and ½ tablespoons sugar
- 1 tablespoon vanilla extract
- 1 egg
- ½ tablespoon apple pie spice
- 1 cup white flour
- ½ tablespoon baking powder
- ½ tablespoon butter, melted

Directions:
In a bowl mix eggs with butter, pie spice, vanilla, apples, sugar, and stir using your mixer. In another bowl, mix baking powder with flour, stir, add to apples mix, stir again well, transfer to your slow cooker, cover, cook on High for 2 hours and 30 minutes, and leave cake aside to cool down, slice and serve.
Enjoy!

Nutrition: calories 200, fat 2, fiber 1, carbs 5, protein 4

Peach Cobbler

Preparation time: 10 minutes
Cooking time: 4 hours
Servings: 2

Ingredients:
- 2 cups peaches, peeled and sliced
- 3 tablespoons sugar
- ½ teaspoon cinnamon powder
- 1 cup sweet crackers, crushed
- ¼ teaspoon nutmeg, ground
- ¼ cup milk
- 1 teaspoon vanilla extract
- Cooking spray

Directions:
In a bowl, mix peaches with half of the sugar and cinnamon and stir. In another bowl, mix crackers with the rest of the sugar, nutmeg, almond milk and vanilla extract and stir. Spray your slow cooker with cooking spray, spread peaches on the bottom, and add crackers mix, spread, cover and cook on Low for 4 hours. Divide cobbler between plates and serve.
Enjoy!

Nutrition: calories 212, fat 4, fiber 4, carbs 7, protein 3

Blueberry and Almond Cake

Preparation time: 10 minutes
Cooking time: 1 hour
Servings: 2

Ingredients:
- ¼ cup flour
- ¼ teaspoon baking powder
- ¼ teaspoon sugar
- ¼ cup blueberries
- ½ cup milk
- 1 teaspoon olive oil
- ½ teaspoon lemon zest, grated
- ¼ teaspoon vanilla extract
- ¼ teaspoon lemon extract
- Cooking spray

Directions:
In a bowl, mix flour with baking powder and sugar and stir. Add blueberries, milk, oil, lemon zest, vanilla extract and lemon extract and whisk well. Spray your slow cooker with cooking spray, line it with parchment paper, pour cake batter, cover pot and cook on High for 1 hour. Leave cake to cool down, slice and serve.
Enjoy!

Nutrition: calories 200, fat 4, fiber 4, carbs 10, protein 4

Pears and Sauce

Preparation time: 10 minutes
Cooking time: 4 hours
Servings: 2

Ingredients:
- 2 pears, peeled and cored
- 1 cup orange juice
- 2 tablespoons maple syrup
- 1 teaspoon cinnamon powder
- ½ tablespoon ginger, grated

Directions:
In your slow cooker, mix pears with orange juice, maple syrup, cinnamon and ginger, cover and cook on Low for 4 hours. Divide pears and sauce between plates and serve warm.
Enjoy!

Nutrition: calories 250, fat 1, fiber 2, carbs 12, protein 4

Almond Cookies

Preparation time: 10 minutes
Cooking time: 2 hours and 30 minutes
Servings: 2

Ingredients:
- 1 tablespoon vegetable oil
- 2 eggs
- ¼ cup sugar
- ¼ teaspoon vanilla extract
- ¼ teaspoon baking powder
- 1 cup flour
- ¼ cup almonds, chopped

Directions:
In a bowl, mix oil with sugar, vanilla extract and eggs and whisk. Add baking powder, almond meal and almonds and stir well. Line your slow cooker with parchment paper, spread cookie mix on the bottom of the pot, cover, and cook on Low for 2 hours and 30 minutes, leave aside to cool down, cut into medium pieces and serve.
Enjoy!

Nutrition: calories 220, fat 2, fiber 1, carbs 6, protein 6

Strawberries and Raisins Marmalade

Preparation time: 10 minutes
Cooking time: 4 hours
Servings: 2

Ingredients:
- 5 ounces strawberries, chopped
- ¼ pound sugar
- Zest of ½ lemon, grated
- 1 ounce raisins
- 1.5 ounces water

Directions:
In your slow cooker, mix strawberries with sugar, lemon zest, raisins and water, stir, cover and cook on High for 4 hours. Divide into small jars and serve cold.
Enjoy!

Nutrition: calories 250, fat 3, fiber 2, carbs 6, protein 1

Easy Lemon Jam

Preparation time: 10 minutes
Cooking time: 3 hours
Servings: 2

Ingredients:
- ½ pound lemons, washed, peeled and sliced
- ½ pounds sugar
- ¼ tablespoon vinegar

Directions:
In your slow cooker, mix lemons with sugar and vinegar, stir, cover, cook on High for 3 hours, divide into jars and serve cold.
Enjoy!

Nutrition: calories 170, fat 0, fiber 2, carbs 7, protein 4

Cinnamon Rice Pudding

Preparation time: 10 minutes
Cooking time: 5 hours
Servings: 4

Ingredients:
- 3 cups water
- ½ cup sugar
- 1 cup white rice
- 1 cinnamon sticks
- ¼ cup coconut, shredded

Directions:
In your slow cooker, mix water with sugar, rice, cinnamon and coconut, stir, cover, cook on High for 5 hours, divide pudding into cups and serve.
Enjoy!

Nutrition: calories 213, fat 4, fiber 6, carbs 10, protein 4

Blueberry Pudding

Preparation time: 10 minutes
Cooking time: 3 hours
Servings: 2

Ingredients:
- ½ cup flour
- 1 tablespoon lemon juice
- 1 cup blueberries
- 1 teaspoons baking powder
- ¼ teaspoon nutmeg, ground
- ¼ cup milk
- ½ cup sugar
- 1 egg, whisked
- 2 tablespoons butter, melted
- ¼ teaspoon vanilla extract
- ½ tablespoon cornstarch
- ½ cup hot water
- Cooking spray

Directions:
Grease your slow cooker with cooking spray, add blueberries and lemon juice, toss and spread them evenly on the bottom of the pot. In a bowl, mix flour with nutmeg, half of the sugar, baking powder, egg, vanilla, butter and milk, whisk well and pour over blueberries. In a small bowl, mix the rest of the sugar with cornstarch and hot water and stir really well. Pour this into your slow cooker as well, cover, cook on High for 3 hours, leave pudding to cool down a bit, divide into bowls and serve
Enjoy!

Nutrition: calories 220, fat 4, fiber 4, carbs 9, protein 6

Almond and Mandarin Pudding

Preparation time: 10 minutes
Cooking time: 2 hours and 30 minutes
Servings: 2

Ingredients:
- ½ mandarin, sliced
- Juice of 1 mandarin
- 1 tablespoon sugar
- 2 ounces butter, soft
- 1 egg
- ½ cup sugar
- ½ cup flour
- ½ teaspoon baking powder
- ½ cup almonds, ground
- Cooking spray

Directions:
Grease your slow cooker with cooking spray, sprinkle half of the sugar on the bottom and arrange mandarin slices. In a bowl, mix butter with the rest of the sugar, egg, almonds, flour, baking powder and the mandarin juice and whisk well. Spread this over mandarin slices, cover, cook on High for 2 hours and 30 minutes, transfer to a platter and serve cold.
Enjoy!

Nutrition: calories 200, fat 4, fiber 2, carbs 8, protein 6

Cinnamon Rolls

Preparation time: 10 minutes
Cooking time: 3 hours
Servings: 2

Ingredients:
- ¼ teaspoon cinnamon powder
- 3 ounces cinnamon roll dough, cut into quarters
- 1 egg
- ¼ cup heavy cream
- Cooking spray
- 1 tablespoon maple syrup
- ½ teaspoon nutmeg, ground
- ½ teaspoons vanilla extract
- 2 tablespoons pecans, chopped

Directions:
Grease your slow cooker with cooking spray and add cinnamon roll pieces. In a bowl, mix egg with cream, vanilla, nutmeg, maple syrup and cinnamon, stir; spread this over cinnamon rolls, sprinkle pecans on top, cover and cook on Low for 3 hours. Divide between plates and serve cinnamon rolls warm.
Enjoy!

Nutrition: calories 200, fat 3, fiber 4, carbs 10, protein 9

Sweet Plums

Preparation time: 10 minutes
Cooking time: 3 hours
Servings: 2

Ingredients:
- 6 plums, halved and pitted
- ½ cup sugar
- 1 teaspoon cinnamon, ground
- ¼ cup water
- 1 tablespoon cornstarch

Directions:
Put plums in your slow cooker, add sugar, cinnamon, water and cornstarch, stir, cover and cook on Low for 3 hours. Divide into small jars and serve as a dessert.
Enjoy!

Nutrition: calories 180, fat 2, fiber 1, carbs 8, protein 8

Plum Cream

Preparation time: 10 minutes
Cooking time: 7 hours
Servings: 2

Ingredients:
- 1 and ½ pounds plums, pitted and halved
- ½ cup water
- ¼ teaspoon cinnamon, ground
- ¼ teaspoon cardamom, ground
- ¼ cup sugar

Directions:
Put plums and water in your slow cooker, cover and cook on Low for 1 hour. Add cinnamon, sugar and cardamom, stir, cover, cook on Low for 6 hours more, divide into jars and serve.
Enjoy!

Nutrition: calories 280, fat 2, fiber 1, carbs 10, protein 6

Sweet Rhubarb Mix

Preparation time: 10 minutes
Cooking time: 6 hours
Servings: 4

Ingredients:
- 2 cups rhubarb, chopped
- 1 tablespoon butter, melted
- ¼ cup water
- ½ cup sugar
- ½ teaspoon vanilla extract

Directions:
Put rhubarb in your slow cooker, add water and sugar, stir gently, cover and cook on Low for 6 hours. Add butter and vanilla, stir and keep in the fridge until its cold.
Enjoy!

Nutrition: calories 200, fat 2, fiber 3, carbs 6, protein 1

Peaches and Special Sauce

Preparation time: 10 minutes
Cooking time: 2 hours
Servings: 2

Ingredients:
- ½ cup brown sugar
- 1 and ½ cups peaches, pitted and cut into wedges
- 3 tablespoons whiskey
- ½ cup white sugar
- 1 teaspoon lemon zest, grated

Directions:
In your slow cooker, mix peaches with brown and white sugar, whiskey and lemon zest, stir, cover and cook on High for 2 hours. Divide into bowls and serve warm.
Enjoy!

Nutrition: calories 200, fat 4, fiber 6, carbs 9, protein 4

Apricot Jam

Preparation time: 10 minutes
Cooking time: 4 hours
Servings: 2

Ingredients:
- 1.5 ounces apricots, and halved
- 1 cup water
- ½ cup sugar
- 1 teaspoon vanilla extract

Directions:
In your slow cooker mix apricots with water, sugar and vanilla, stir, cover and cook on Low for 4 hours. Divide into bowls and serve.
Enjoy!

Nutrition: calories 200, fat 4, fiber 5, carbs 10, protein 4

Black Grapes Dessert

Preparation time: 10 minutes
Cooking time: 2 hours
Servings: 2

Ingredients:
- 2 ounces black grapes
- ¼ cup water
- 1 and ½ tablespoons sugar
- ½ cup corn flour
- 1 teaspoon lemon juice

Directions:
Put grapes in your slow cooker, add water, sugar, flour and lemon juice, stir, cover and cook on Low for 2 hours. Stir again well, divide into bowls and serve.
Enjoy!

Nutrition: calories 100, fat 3, fiber 6, carbs 8, protein 3

Pomegranate Jam

Preparation time: 10 minutes
Cooking time: 3 hours
Servings: 2

Ingredients:
- 2 and ½ cups pomegranate seeds
- ¼ cup pomegranate juice
- 1 tablespoon lemon juice
- ½ cup white sugar

Directions:
In your slow cooker, mix pomegranate seeds with juice, lemon juice and sugar, stir, cover and cook on Low for 3 hours. Divide into bowls and serve cold.
Enjoy!

Nutrition: calories 162, fat 4, fiber 5, carbs 20, protein 6

Sweet Orange Cream

Preparation time: 10 minutes
Cooking time: 2 hours
Servings: 2

Ingredients:
- ½ teaspoon ginger paste
- 3 tablespoons sugar
- ½ cup orange juice
- 3 oranges, peeled and chopped
- 2 tablespoons agave nectar
- 2 tablespoons cornstarch

Directions:
In you're your slow cooker, mix oranges with orange juice, ginger, sugar, agave nectar and corn flour, stir well, cover and cook on High for 2 hours. Stir your cream one more time, divide into bowls and serve cold.
Enjoy!

Nutrition: calories 100, fat 4, fiber 5, carbs 6, protein 7

Cranberries and Clementine Cream

Preparation time: 10 minutes
Cooking time: 1 hour
Servings: 2

Ingredients:
- 5 ounces cranberries
- ½ cup water
- flesh and peel from 1 clementine
- ½ cup sugar

Directions:
In your slow cooker, mix cranberries with clementine juice and flesh, water and sugar, stir, cover and cook on High for 1 hour. Divide into bowls and serve cold.
Enjoy!

Nutrition: calories 100, fat 3, fiber 6, carbs 7, protein 3

Sweet Pineapple Mix

Preparation time: 10 minutes
Cooking time: 1 hour
Servings: 2

Ingredients:
- 1 and ½ cups pineapple cubes
- 1 and ½ tablespoons rum
- 1 and ½ tablespoons butter
- 2 tablespoons brown sugar
- ½ teaspoon cinnamon powder
- ½ teaspoon allspice, ground
- ½ teaspoon nutmeg, ground
- ½ teaspoon ginger, grated

Directions:
In your slow cooker, mix pineapple with butter, rum, sugar, cinnamon, allspice, nutmeg and ginger, stir, cover and cook on High for 1 hour. Divide into bowls and serve cold.
Enjoy!

Nutrition: calories 152, fat 3, fiber 1, carbs 17, protein 3

Strawberry Mix

Preparation time: 10 minutes
Cooking time: 1 hour
Servings: 2

Ingredients:
- 2 tablespoons orange juice
- 3 tablespoons sugar
- ¼ pound strawberries, halved
- A pinch of ginger powder
- ½ teaspoon vanilla extract

Directions:
In your slow cooker, mix strawberries with sugar, orange juice, ginger and vanilla, stir, cover and cook on High for 1 hour. Divide into bowls and serve cold.
Enjoy!

Nutrition: calories 100, fat 2, fiber 2, carbs 10, protein 2

Cranberry Mix

Preparation time: 10 minutes
Cooking time: 1 hour
Servings: 2

Ingredients:
- 2 teaspoons orange zest
- 6 ounces cranberries
- 2 tablespoons orange juice
- 1 tablespoon maple syrup
- ½ cup sugar

Directions:
In your slow cooker, mix cranberries with orange zest, orange juice, maple syrup and sugar, stir, cover and cook on High for 1 hour. Divide into bowls and serve cold
Enjoy!

Nutrition: calories 123, fat 1, fiber 2, carbs 20, protein 3

Sweet Melon Dessert

Preparation time: 5 minutes
Cooking time: 1 hour
Servings: 2

Ingredients:
- Flesh from 2 small melons
- 2 tablespoons sugar
- 3 tablespoons sweet wine
- 1 tablespoon butter
- 1 teaspoon cornstarch
- Juice of ½ lemon

Directions:
In your slow cooker, mix melon with sugar, wine, butter, cornstarch and lemon juice, stir, cover and cook on High for 1 hour. Divide into bowls and serve cold.
Enjoy!

Nutrition: calories 100, fat 2, fiber 3, carbs 6, protein 1

Chocolate Cheesecake

Preparation time: 1 hour
Cooking time: 4 hours
Servings: 2

Ingredients:
For the crust:
- 1 tablespoon melted butter
- ½ cup chocolate cookies, crumbled

For the filling:
- 6 ounces cream cheese, soft
- ½ tablespoon cornstarch
- ¼ cup sugar
- 1 egg
- ¼ tablespoon vanilla extract
- Cooking spray
- 2 tablespoons Greek yogurt
- 1 ounce white chocolate
- 1 ounce bittersweet chocolate

Directions:
In a bowl mix cookie crumbs with butter and stir well. Grease your slow cooker with the cooking oil, line with parchment paper and press crumbs and butter mix on the bottom. In a bowl, mix cream cheese with cornstarch and sugar and stir using your mixer. Add egg, yogurt and vanilla, stir again to combine everything and divide into 2 bowls. Put dark and white chocolate in 2 heatproof bowls and heat them up in the microwave for 30 seconds. Add these to the 2 bowls with cheesecake batter, stir and introduce them all in the fridge for 30 minutes. Take bowls out of the fridge and layer your cheesecake. Pour the dark chocolate batter into the center of the crust. Add white chocolate batter on top, spread evenly, cover pot and cook on Low for 4 hours. Take cake out of the pot, leave aside to cool down and serve.
Enjoy!

Nutrition: calories 276, fat 12, fiber 3, carbs 20, protein 4

Chocolate Cream

Preparation time: 10 minutes
Cooking time: 30 minutes
Servings: 2

Ingredients:
- 1.5 ounces crème fraiche
- 1.5 ounces dark chocolate, cut into chunks
- ½ teaspoon liquor
- ½ teaspoon sugar

Directions:
In a heatproof container that fits your slow cooker, mix chocolate chunks with sugar, crème fraiche and liquor. Add this to your slow cooker, cover, cook on Low for 30 minutes, stir again really well and serve right away with some fresh berries.
Enjoy!

Nutrition: calories 200, fat 12, fiber 4, carbs 7, protein 3

Tasty Blackberry Jam

Preparation time: 10 minutes
Cooking time: 3 hours
Servings: 2

Ingredients:
- ½ cup blackberries
- ¼ cup sugar
- ¼ teaspoon allspice, ground
- A pinch of cinnamon powder
- ½ teaspoon lemon juice
- ½ tablespoon cornstarch

Directions:
In your slow cooker, mix blackberries with sugar, allspice, cinnamon, lemon juice and cornstarch, stir, cover, cook on Low for 3 hours, divide into cups and serve cold.
Enjoy!

Nutrition: calories 70, fat 1, fiber 3, carbs 13, protein 1

Spiced Peach Jam

Preparation time: 10 minutes
Cooking time: 3 hours
Servings: 2

Ingredients:
- 1 cup peaches, peeled and chopped
- ½ cup sugar
- ½ tablespoon lemon juice
- A pinch of allspice
- A pinch of cinnamon powder

Directions:
In your slow cooker, mix peaches with sugar, lemon juice, allspice and cinnamon, stir, cover and cook on Low for 3 hours. Blend using an immersion blender, divide into cups and serve cold.
Enjoy!

Nutrition: calories 50, fat 0, fiber 2, carbs 10, protein 0

Rhubarb Jam

Preparation time: 10 minutes
Cooking time: 3 hours
Servings: 2

Ingredients:
- ½ pound rhubarb, chopped
- ½ cup sugar
- ½ teaspoon orange zest
- 3 tablespoons orange juice
- ¼ cup water

Directions:
In your slow cooker, mix rhubarb with sugar, orange zest, orange juice and water, stir, cover and cook on Low for 3 hours. Stir jam well, divide into bowls and serve cold.
Enjoy!

Nutrition: calories 60, fat 1, fiber 0, carbs 10, protein 1

Strawberry Jam

Preparation time: 10 minutes
Cooking time: 3 hours
Servings: 2

Ingredients:
- ½ pound strawberries, halved
- 2 tablespoons lemon juice
- 1 cup sugar

Directions:
In your slow cooker, mix strawberries with lemon juice and sugar, stir, cover and cook on Low for 3 hours. Stir jam again, divide into bowls and serve cold.
Enjoy!

Nutrition: calories 90, fat 1, fiber 2, carbs 20, protein 1

Pear and Honey Jam

Preparation time: 10 minutes
Cooking time: 3 hours
Servings: 2

Ingredients:
- ½ pound pears, peeled and cut into medium wedges
- ½ cup honey
- 2 ounces canned pineapple and juice
- Juice of ½ lemon

Directions:
In your slow cooker, mix pears with honey, pineapple and juice and lemon juice, stir, cover and cook on Low for 3 hours. Divide into cups and serve cold.
Enjoy!

Nutrition: calories 134, fat 1, fiber 3, carbs 20, protein 1

Lingo berry Jam

Preparation time: 10 minutes
Cooking time: 2 hours
Servings: 2

Ingredients:
- ½ pound lingo berries
- ¼ cup sugar
- 1 cup water

Directions:
In your slow cooker, mix lingo berries with sugar and water, stir, cover and cook on Low for 2 hours. Divide into bowls and serve cold.
Enjoy!

Nutrition: calories 40, fat 0, fiber 1, carbs 10, protein 1

Strawberry and Jalapeno Marmalade

Preparation time: 10 minutes
Cooking time: 3 hours
Servings: 2

Ingredients:
- 1 cup strawberries, halved
- ¼ cup jalapenos, minced
- 2 tablespoons lemon juice
- 1 teaspoon fruit pectin
- 2 cups sugar

Directions:
In your slow cooker, mix strawberries with jalapenos, lemon juice, pectin and sugar, stir, cover and cook on Low for 3 hours. Stir again, divide into bowls and serve cold.
Enjoy!

Nutrition: calories 100, fat 1, fiber 2, carbs 20, protein 1

Spicy Tomato Jam

Preparation time: 10 minutes
Cooking time: 4 hours
Servings: 2

Ingredients:
- ½ pound tomatoes, peeled and chopped
- 2 tablespoons apple cider vinegar
- 1 tablespoon lemon juice
- 1 apple, peeled and chopped
- 3 tablespoons sugar
- A pinch of cayenne
- 2 tablespoons brown sugar

Directions:
In your slow cooker, mix tomatoes with vinegar, lemon juice, apple, white sugar, brown sugar and cayenne, stir, cover and cook on Low for 4 hours. Divide into cups and serve cold.
Enjoy!

Nutrition: calories 60, fat 1, fiber 2, carbs 20, protein 1

Chili Jam

Preparation time: 10 minutes
Cooking time: 3 hours
Servings: 2

Ingredients:
- 3 jalapenos, halved
- 1 tomato, chopped
- 1 green apple, grated
- 2 tablespoons red wine vinegar
- 3 tablespoons sugar

Directions:
In your slow cooker, mix jalapenos with tomato, apple, vinegar and sugar, stir, cover and cook on Low for 3 hours. Stir jam, divide into bowls and serve cold.
Enjoy!

Nutrition: calories 70, fat 1, fiber 1, carbs 18, protein 1

Onion Jam

Preparation time: 10 minutes
Cooking time: 3 hours
Servings: 2

Ingredients:
- 1 cup sweet onions, chopped
- 2 tablespoons vegetable oil
- 1 tablespoon red wine vinegar
- 4 tablespoons sugar
- A pinch of salt

Directions:
In your slow cooker, mix sweet onions with oil, vinegar, sugar and a pinch of salt, cover and cook on Low for 3 hours. Stir well, divide into bowls and serve cold.
Enjoy!

Nutrition: calories 40, fat 1, fiber 1, carbs 5, protein 0

Different Tomato Jam

Preparation time: 10 minutes
Cooking time: 3 hours
Servings: 2

Ingredients:
- ½ pound tomatoes, chopped
- 1 cup hot water
- 4 tablespoons apple juice
- ¼ teaspoon black pepper
- 3 tablespoons sugar
- 1 tablespoon cider vinegar
- A pinch of allspice, ground

Directions:
In your slow cooker, mix tomatoes with water, apple juice, sugar, black pepper, vinegar and allspice, stir, cover and cook on Low for 3 hours. Stir jam again, divide into bowls and serve cold.
Enjoy!

Nutrition: calories 50, fat 1, fiber 1, carbs 10, protein 2

Bread Pudding

Preparation time: 10 minutes
Cooking time: 3 hours
Servings: 2

Ingredients:
- 4 cups bread, cubed
- ½ cup raisins
- 2 tablespoons butter, melted
- 2 tablespoons white sugar
- 1 cup milk
- 2 eggs
- A pinch of nutmeg, ground
- ¼ teaspoon vanilla extract

Directions:
In your slow cooker, mix bread with raisins. In a bowl, mix eggs with milk, butter, sugar, vanilla and nutmeg, stir, pour over bread mix, cover pot and cook on Low for 3 hours. Divide pudding between plates and serve.
Enjoy!

Nutrition: calories 354, fat 12, fiber 4, carbs 29, protein 11

Tapioca Pudding

Preparation time: 10 minutes
Cooking time: 2 hours and 30 minutes
Servings: 2

Ingredients:
- 1 cup milk
- ¼ cup tapioca pears
- 1 egg yolk
- ½ teaspoon vanilla extract
- 3 tablespoons sugar

Directions:
In your slow cooker, mix tapioca with sugar, milk and vanilla, stir, cover and cook on High for 2 hours. In a bowl, whisk egg yolk with 1 tablespoon of hot mix from the pot, add to your pudding, stir, cover and cook on High for 30 minutes more. Divide pudding into bowls and serve cold.
Enjoy!

Nutrition: calories 180, fat 3, fiber 4, carbs 12, protein 4

Conclusion

We know you are constantly looking for great and delicious recipes to prepare for you and your loved one and that's why we developed this cooking journal.
As you now know, this recipes collection is a pretty special one!
You not only get some of the best recipes in the world!
You get the best ones you can cook in your slow cooker!
How cool is that?

Don't wait too long! Get a copy of this amazing cookbook and start making the best meals in your life for you and your loved one using just your slow cooker!
You will be admired and appreciated for your cooking skills for sure!
Enjoy!

Recipe Index

A
Almond And Beans Spread, 97
Almond And Mandarin Pudding, 120
Almond Cookies, 117
Almond Snack, 96
Amazing German Oatmeal, 17
Apple And Cashew Butter Bowls, 27
Apple Cake, 115
Apple Dip, 105
Apple Pie Oatmeal, 16
Apples And Pears Bowls, 26
Apricot Jam, 123
Artichokes Party Spread, 85
Asian Salmon Fillets, 35

B
Bacon Chili, 51
Baked Beans, 74
Baked Egg Casserole, 19
Balsamic Chicken Mix, 55
Banana Cake, 111
BBQ Short Ribs, 52
Beans And Sauce, 72
Beans And Spinach Mix, 65
Beans Breakfast Burrito, 32
Beef And Artichoke Soup, 57
Beef Cakes, 103
Beef Party Meatballs, 100
Beef Stew, 44
Berry And Cashew Cake, 113
Berry Butter, 33
Black Grapes Dessert, 123
Blueberry And Almond Cake, 116
Blueberry And Banana Oatmeal, 14
Blueberry Pudding, 119
Bread Pudding, 134
Breakfast Casserole, 12
Breakfast Pork Meatloaf, 29
Breakfast Potatoes Mix, 10
Breakfast Pumpkin Spread, 31
Bulgur Appetizer Salad, 94
Butternut Mix, 64

C
Cabbage And Apples Mix, 75
Caesar Artichoke Dip, 85
Carrot Oatmeal, 15
Carrots And Zucchini Oatmeal, 13
Cashew And Coconut Pudding, 113
Cashew Spread, 87
Cauliflower And Broccoli Mix, 66
Cauliflower Dip, 108
Cauliflower Mash, 79
Cheese And Veggies Casserole, 26
Cheesy Crab Dip, 86
Cheesy Mushroom Salsa, 92
Cheesy Spinach, 78
Cherry And Cocoa Compote, 112
Cherry Oats, 31
Chicken And Mushrooms, 39
Chicken Chili, 39
Chicken Dip, 109
Chicken Drumsticks And Blue Cheese Sauce, 56
Chicken Meatballs, 106
Chicken Soup, 49
Chickpeas Appetizer Salad, 93
Chili Black Beans Mix, 69
Chili Jam, 132
Chocolate Cheesecake, 127
Chocolate Cream, 128
Cinnamon Plum Compote, 115
Cinnamon Rice Pudding, 119
Cinnamon Rolls, 120
Clam Chowder, 38
Coconut And Chocolate Cream, 111
Coconut Clams, 37
Corn Chowder, 63
Corn Dip, 91
Cornbread Breakfast Mix, 34
Crab And Artichoke Spread, 86
Cranberries And Clementine Cream, 125
Cranberry Mix, 126
Cranberry Oatmeal, 15
Creamy Apples, 114
Creamy Banana Breakfast, 12
Creamy Beef Mix, 46
Creamy Corn Side Dish, 62
Creamy Mushroom Appetizer, 94
Creamy Oatmeal, 10
Creamy Potatoes, 65
Creamy Scalloped Tater Tots, 60
Curried Veggie Side Dish, 67

D
Delicious Bean Mix, 61
Delicious Chicken And Rice, 54
Delicious Potato Omelet, 21
Different Tomato Jam, 133

E
Easy And Tasty Tacos, 96
Easy Banana Bread, 24
Easy Green Beans Mix, 61
Easy Leeks And Fennel Soup, 57
Easy Lemon Jam, 118
Easy Pecans Snack, 101
Easy Potatoes Mix, 64
Eggplant Appetizer Salad, 99
Eggplant Salsa, 97
Eggplant Stew, 58
Eggs And Bacon Breakfast Mix, 30

F

Fish Sticks, 101
Flavored Mushroom Mix, 76
Flavored Potato And Spinach Mix, 73
French Chicken Dish, 51

H
Hash Brown Breakfast, 11
Honey Roast, 46
Hot Beans, 73
Hot Beans And Lentils, 70
Hummus, 89

I
Indian Chicken, 40
Italian Eggplant Mix, 84
Italian Pork Loin, 50
Italian Veggie Dip, 89

K
Kale Frittata, 22

L
Lamb Stew, 43
Leek, Kale And Sausage Casserole, 29
Lemon Chicken, 48
Lentils Dip, 99
Lentils Sloppy Joe, 95
Lentils Soup, 47
Lentils Stew, 59
Light Peanut Butter Oatmeal, 14
Lingo berry Jam, 131
Lovely Quinoa Breakfast Mix, 11

M
Maple And Thyme Brussels Sprouts, 68
Mashed Potatoes, 71
Mexican Frittata, 22
Mexican Rice Breakfast, 32
Mini Sausages Snack, 109
Mixed Pork, Beef And Beans, 54
Mixed Veggies Side Dish, 75
Moroccan Risotto, 81
Mushroom Rice, 63
Mushroom Risotto, 67
Mustard Pork Chops, 56

N
Nuts And Squash Bowls, 27

O
Onion Dip, 98
Onion Jam, 133

P
Parmesan And Peas Rice, 82
Peach Bowls, 20
Peach Cobbler, 116
Peaches And Special Sauce, 122
Pear And Honey Jam, 130
Pear And Maple Oatmeal, 25
Pears And Sauce, 117
Pecans Snack, 107

Pineapple Rice, 83
Plum Cream, 121
Pomegranate Jam, 124
Pork And Apples, 43
Pork And Eggs Breakfast Mix, 28
Pork Chops And Creamy Sauce, 55
Pork Chops And Pineapple Mix, 42
Pork Roast And Veggies, 44
Potato And Bacon Soup, 53
Potato Casserole, 25
Potato Salad, 90
Potatoes And Apples Mix, 69
Pulled Chicken, 38
Pumpkin Bread, 24
Pumpkin Butter, 33
Pumpkin Oatmeal, 16

Q
Quick Broccoli Side Dish, 60
Quinoa Casserole, 17
Quinoa Pilaf, 80
Quinoa Pudding, 34

R
Refried Beans Spread, 92
Rhubarb Jam, 129
Rice And Farro Pilaf, 80
Rich Breakfast Casserole, 19
Roasted Beef Chuck, 42
Root Veggie Salad, 95
Rosemary Potatoes, 68

S
Sausage Bites, 102
Sausage Casserole, 28
Scallops And Shrimp Stew, 36
Seafood Chowder, 35
Seafood Salad, 104
Seasoned Peanuts, 107
Shrimp Breakfast Casserole, 20
Simple Artichokes, 83
Simple Bok Choy, 84
Simple Carrots Mix, 70
Simple Citrus Pudding, 114
Simple Flavored Salmon, 37
Simple Kale Side Dish, 77
Simple Nuts Snack, 98
Simple Sweet Potatoes Mix, 78
Slow Cooked Beef Stew And Red Wine, 45
Slow Cooked Chicken, 41
Slow Cooked Chicken Mix, 48
Slow Cooked Pasta Dish, 45
Smooth Beef Brisket, 52
Special Omelet, 21
Spiced Peach Jam, 129
Spicy Tomato Jam, 132
Spicy Tuna, 36
Spinach And Cheese Rice, 82

Spinach And Mushroom Tortellini, 50
Spinach Breakfast Quiche, 23
Spinach Dip, 90
Spinach Spread, 102
Squash And Sauce, 76
Squash Mix, 72
Squash Salad, 106
Squash Spread, 87
Squid Appetizer, 103
Strawberries And Raisins Marmalade, 118
Strawberry And Jalapeno Marmalade, 131
Strawberry Jam, 130
Strawberry Mix, 126
Stuffed Apples, 110
Stuffed Bell Peppers, 91
Stuffed Chicken Appetizer, 104
Stuffed Jalapenos, 100
Sweet Apples And Cane Juice, 110
Sweet Melon Dessert, 127
Sweet Orange Cream, 124
Sweet Pineapple Mix, 125
Sweet Plums, 121
Sweet Potato Casserole, 30
Sweet Potato Dip, 105
Sweet Potatoes And Orange Mix, 66
Sweet Rhubarb Mix, 122

T

Tapioca Pudding, 134
Tasty Blackberry Jam, 128
Tasty Breakfast Pie, 18
Tasty Cauliflower Hash Browns, 18
Tasty Gumbo, 49
Tasty Peas And Carrots, 62
Tater Tot Casserole, 13
Thai Tofu Party Mix, 93
Turkey And Chickpeas Stew, 47
Turkey And Sweet Potatoes, 41
Turkey With Cherries, Cranberries And Figs, 40

V

Veggie Mix, 79
Veggie Party Rolls, 88
Veggie Spread, 88
Veggie Stew, 58

W

Walnuts And Pumpkin Seeds Snack, 108
White Bean Mix, 74
White Chicken Soup, 53
Wild Rice Mix, 71
Winter Pudding, 112

Z

Zucchini And Squash Mix, 77
Zucchini Frittata, 23

Copyright 2017 by Steven D Shaw All rights reserved.

All rights Reserved. No part of this publication or the information in it may be quoted from or reproduced in any form by means such as printing, scanning, photocopying or otherwise without prior written permission of the copyright holder.

Disclaimer and Terms of Use: Effort has been made to ensure that the information in this book is accurate and complete, however, the author and the publisher do not warrant the accuracy of the information, text and graphics contained within the book due to the rapidly changing nature of science, research, known and unknown facts and internet. The Author and the publisher do not hold any responsibility for errors, omissions or contrary interpretation of the subject matter herein. This book is presented solely for motivational and informational purposes only.

Made in the USA
Coppell, TX
09 November 2019